# DATE DUE

| | | | |
|---|---|---|---|
| ~~OC 7 02~~ | | | |
| ~~FE 3 05~~ | | | |
| FE 10 05 | | | |
| ~~MR 8 05~~ | | | |
| ~~MR 28 05~~ | | | |
| ~~AP 25 05~~ | | | |
| OC 7 09 | | | |
| FE 11 10 | | | |
| | | | |
| | | | |
| | | | |
| | | | |
| | | | |
| | | | |
| | | | |
| | | | |

# GOD IS A WOMAN

# gender
## in crisis

series editor, montana katz, ph.d.

We are fitfully and certainly moving away from a world in which women are defined as less than men, where masculinity and femininity are separate realms of experience. It is clear that gender will no longer be as determining a factor to an individual's personal identity, choices, and aspirations as it once was. This cultural shift will affect every aspect of life, from subtle daily details to broad social principles. The Gender in Crisis Series explores the future meaning, construction, and impact of gender on all of our lives.

The Gender Bias Prevention Book:
Helping Girls and Women to Have
Satisfying Lives and Careers
*Montana Katz*

God is a Woman
*Rafael López-Corvo*

# GOD IS A WOMAN

## Rafael E. López-Corvo

**JASON ARONSON INC.**
*Northvale, NJ*
*London*

Director of Editorial Production: Robert D. Hack

This book was set in 10 pt. Bookman by TechType of Ramsey, NJ, and printed and bound by Book-mart Press, Inc. of North Bergen, NJ.

**Library of Congress Cataloging-in-Publication Data**

López-Corvo, Rafael E.
    God is a woman / Rafael E. López-Corvo.
      p.   cm.
   Includes bibliographical references and index.
   ISBN 1-56821-862-1 (hc : alk. paper)
    1. Women and religion.  2. Femininity of God.  I. Title.
  BL458.L66  1996
  305.42—dc20                         96-15630

Printed in the United States of America on acid-free paper. For information and catalog write to Jason Aronson Inc., 230 Livingston Street, Northvale, New Jersey 07647-1731. Or visit our website: http://www.aronson.com

# CONTENTS

TO ALL WOMEN,
especially those with whom I have shared my life

# INTRODUCTION

Although it is quite possible that many will consider this book irreverent or disrespectful of ideas or institutions, I am certain that they will also perceive it as a defender of women and their unquestionable transcendence throughout history. The main ideas I now share publicly are ones I have considered for many years: the classification of the "Eves," the masochistic character of women, the concept of "giraffe women," and so forth. Other ideas appeared afterwards, some at the last moment as I enjoyed the company of friends, who frequently and generously lent their time to discuss with me their own opinions.

The central issue I am introducing now consists of the idea that a great majority of the developments that humanity has had, and will achieve in the future, depend on three main sources:

a) New discoveries in biology;
b) The electronic shrinking of the earth, in a Marshall McLuhan sense; and
c) Women's own capacity to change—not men's, but women's—for, in a sort of spiral evolution, as women mutate, they will also help men to grow. After all, they are the ones to whom we were attached during the tenderest and most influential moments of our life.

I have represented this progress of women according to three main stages of evolution. The first one comprises the period between the beginning of time to the present century, when the women's liberation movement started to take place. I have given this stage the name of the "Delinquent Eve," as a condensation of the woman depicted by the myth of Genesis: plundered of her maternity by a male God, accused of conniving with the devil, and guilty of the eternal loss of Paradise. The second period, believed to be experienced by women now, I have labeled as the "Confused Eve" because I think it represents the need of women to achieve their identity by imitating certain idealized features of men: their apparent freedom, political power, money, external genitality, and so forth. I do not intend, however, by any means to criticize feminist attempts to overcome the pressure of discrimination that men and society at large—including women themselves— have exercised against them for so many years. These movements took place along these lines, meaning the need to imitate men, because fatalistically it was the only way possible. My purpose, which is absolutely descriptive, unbiased, and with honest intentions, is to introduce a hypothesis in order to evaluate what feminist Susan Faludi referred to as the backlash in women's liberation, the recurring failure observed by women searching for their rights in a *confused* way and in the wrong direction: by idealization of men and imitation of those idealized features in a rather difficult sort of love-hate relationship. The future answer is not to give up the struggle, but to change the method and revert the aims. The problem of this "Confused Eve," as I will discuss further in the text, consists of a tendency to look for the answer guided by a fascination of the exterior, the evident, the idealized features of masculinity she has been exposed to for so many years, instead of searching inside of the woman proper, within the mystery of her own femininity, of her own identity; a more difficult and elusive search perhaps, but the correct direction nevertheless. This myopic "phallotropism" of women, such a confusion of aim and direction, is, I believe, the reason for the repetitious backlash in all women's liberation movements that have taken place until now: *"A backlash against women's rights is nothing new in American history,"* says Susan Faludi, *"indeed, it's a recurring phenomenon: it returns every time women begin to make some headway toward equality"* (1991, p. 46). Ann Douglas as well, stated: *"The progress of women's rights in our culture, unlike other types of progress, has always been strangely reversible"* (1977, p. 199); whereas Dale Spender writes: *"While men proceed on their developmental way, building on inherited traditions, women are confined to cycles of lost and found"* (1983, p. 4).

The problem consists in the human proneness towards all too easy outside stimulations instead of an honest, careful, and long-term inner quest. This inclination for outside fascination is perhaps the cause and effect of a profitable industry of superficial, skin deep, weekend-package psychology that attempts to introduce lasting changes in people's personality structures by means of pure imitation, or "as if" type of behavior, rather than by the laborious search inside the depth of our minds, within the unknown profundity of human unconsciousness; because after all, it is easier to blame than to take responsibility. Discussing this last statement, John Taylor recently referred to the "don't blame me culture of victimization":

> *"It is a strange phenomenon," says he, "this growing compulsion of Americans of all creeds, colors, and incomes, of the young and the old, the infirm and the robust, the guilty as well as the innocent, to ascribe to themselves the status of victims to try to find someone or something else to blame for whatever is wrong or incomplete or just plain unpleasant about their lives. . .It is a major theme in race relations and in the feminist critique of society. It has spawned a new academic discipline, victimology."* [1991, p. 28]

But Taylor's culture of victimization is not by any means a new form of rationalization, on the contrary, it could be traced already to the time of Genesis: "And he said [the Lord]. . .Hast thou eaten of the tree, whereof I commanded thee that thou shouldest not eat? And the man said, *The woman whom thou gavest to be with me she gave me of the tree, and I did eat.* And the Lord said unto the woman, What is this that thou hast done? And the woman said, *The serpent beguiled me and I did eat"* (Gen. 3:11–3, italics added).

Taking a different view, Susan Faludi states that "women's advances and retreats are generally described in military terms: battles won, battles lost, points and territory gained and surrendered. . .But imagining the conflict as two battalions neatly arrayed on either side of the line, we miss the entangled nature, the locked embrace of a 'war' between women and the male culture they inhabit" (1991, p. xx). It is not without reason that Mona Charen complained that the feminist movement "has effectively robbed us of one thing upon which the happiness of most women rests—men" (1984, p. 24). Back in the seventies, for instance, feminist Robin Morgan felt the denigration of feminine attributes and identification with male idiosyncrasies were a definite road towards liberation: "I. . .stopped wearing makeup," she said, "and shaving my legs, started learning karate, and changed my politics completely" (1970, p. xvi).

Women had already planted the seed of discontent, had for some time protested the long years of ignominy, and refused to accept the pressure of continuous discrimination; however, just as might happen with any important sociological change—like communism, for example—they could follow the wrong direction, guided by the fascination of a glorified masculinity, instead of looking within the depth of their own selves. Just as "Delinquent Eves" are responsible for the arrival of "macho men," "Confused Eves" are directly responsible for the existence of "confused men," a sort of bisexual male generation seen everywhere at the present, for instance, in the sexual ambiguity of very popular entertainers, such as Madonna, or even the more diffused identity of Michael Jackson, who epitomize all confusions indeed, no longer knowing who he is, whether a he or a she, a black or a white. It is particularly interesting to observe women's dependency manifested in their universal and compulsory need to carry a purse, representing not the symbolism of their own womb, as many have thought, but that of their mother's, like marsupials, where they unconsciously place, in order to secure, their own childhood wishes, dreams, and memories of imitating their mothers and later becoming adults.

To such stupefaction former feminist, and now masculinist, poet Robert Bly, had referred to, during a 1982 written dialogue with colleague Keith Thompson, as the "soft male":

> *Bly: I see the phenomenon of what I would call the "soft male" all over this country today. Sometimes when I look at my audiences, perhaps half the young males are what I'd call soft. . .Thompson: Perhaps it's because back in the sixties, when we looked to the women's movement for leads as how we should be, the message we got was that the new strong women wanted soft men. Bly: I agree. That's how it felt.* [Bly 1982]

And later on during an interview, he states: "I just see it getting worse and worse. Men will become more and more insecure, farther from their own manhood. Men will become more like women, women will try to be more like men. It's not a good prospect."

Although I agree with the definition of the conflict and think that Bly's statement describes with great accuracy the characteristics of this "Confused Eve's" era, I disagree completely with the methodology offered in order to overcome the complications, or to disarrange the malaise induced by the confusion that both male and female seem to endure. Using a sort of weekend marathon psychology, Bly and his associates attempt to repair the "damage" feminists have induced in the new generation of "soft males" by trying to bring out the "wild side," the wild man that most soft males might carry inside. Journalist John Tevlin, who attended one of these encounters back in 1988 at the Bible camp in Mound, Minnesota, relates with certain wit what happened at this meeting led by Shepherd Bliss, one of Bly's followers:

> *As he [Bliss] spoke of recovering the 'wild man within' that first night, Shepherd slowly dropped to his knees. "Some of you may want to temporarily leave the world of the two-leggeds and join me in the world of the four-leggeds," he said. One by one, we slid from our orange Naugahyde chairs onto an orange shag carpet ripped straight out of the 1960s. "You may find yourself behaving like these four-leggeds; you may be scratching the earth, getting in contact with the dirt..." As he spoke, people began pawing at the ground... "You may find yourself behaving like the most masculine of all animals—the ram", Shepherd said in a coaxing voice..."You may find unfamiliar noises emerging from your throats!" ...There were gurgles and bleats, a few wolf calls ...Out of the corner of my eye, I saw Shepherd coming toward me, head down, tufts of white hair ringing a bald spot...Meanwhile, I felt a slight presence at my rear, and turned to see a man beginning to sniff my buttocks. "Woof!" he said. [Tevlin 1989]*

In the same manner that women will not be able to find their own identity by imitating idealized male attributes, neither will males achieve lost macho traits by imitating animals. *Identification* is a complicated developmental process everybody is capable of exercising in order to grow and to achieve internal, competent, and lasting changes, not by imitation like the monkeys, but by real inner transformation, a mechanism only human beings are capable of accomplishing. However, I also understand that out of desperation and confusion the mass tries to find the easiest way out, even if by doing so, like the frog, it might not aim in the right direction and endlessly hit its head against the same wall.

Once women overcome these tremendous difficulties, many years from now, they will finally be able to obtain the power of their own identity. Then, I say, another woman will appear, who I have named the "Vindicated Eve." This exercise will not, in any case, be an easy task; it will require many years of trial and error, of continuous attempts and backlashes.

While I was writing these comments, I discovered that in the late sixties writer Merlin Stone published a book entitled *When God Was A Woman.* From comments she made in the introduction of a more recent publication, *The Goddess Re-awakening,* I find myself moving in a similar direction: *"When I first began seriously researching and writing* When God Was A Woman, *in the late sixties",* she said,

> . . .*my goal was to show how narrow and binding our society's images of women were. We were still functioning on biblical concepts and decrees. All throughout the Old and New Testaments were statements that women should defer to the wishes of men because Eve fed an apple to Adam. The idea that the male should rule over the females was deeply embedded in even the most atheistic minds. Over the centuries, this attitude had been so completely ab-*

> sorbed into the general social outlook that most
> people assumed such a gender stratification was
> simply the natural gender pattern. [1989, p. 2]

Although I agree with most of what has been expressed here, I dissent with the inclination towards idealization of the past, of women previously holding important prerogatives and positions that she then lost due to unknown circumstances, and that she is trying again to recover: that she was a God before, is no longer one now, but is "awakening" again. *"For us to construct such a future [of women],"* said Riane Eisler, *"requires that the feminine principle—so long denied, degraded, and subordinated in both our belief systems and our lives—be reinstated to its rightful place"* (1989, p. 27). I seriously think that trying to find answers in the past is as sad, if not sadder, than trying to find answers through the imitation of men. It seems that "Confused Eve" remains trapped between her longing and tears for an idealized past that never existed, and the frustration and anger against male's idealized attributes impossible to secure: older times are not always better, nor is the neighbor's grass always greener. We cannot search for the answers in the past because history is not circular; a spiral perhaps, but not circular. The future is ahead and unknown; today's time is modern, but tomorrow it will be primitive because we are always manufacturing history.

There is, however, in my opinion, a very important contribution the authors of *The Goddess Re-awakening* are seriously attempting to introduce: the presence of a "universal feminine principle": *". . .as long as the concept of a feminine principle, says Merlin Stone, continues to be used as an underlying premise in theories of psychology, philosophy, and spirituality, affecting the thinking of so many people, we feel that this concept requires long-overdue examination"* (1989, p. 5). I believe that there is a *universal feminine principle* just as there is a masculine one, the difference remains in the fact that, from the very beginning of creation, everything about man has already been said and nothing continues to be undisclosed, whereas woman is an untold story yet to be discovered. Such *feminine principle* must be related with the socio-biological power of *imprinting*, with the guilt that such fatalistic puissance of imprinting induces, together with the apparent complication of an anatomically hidden sexuality. *This essay will attempt to define the aforementioned feminine principle, to evaluate the obstacles that obstruct woman's road towards self-illumination, and to likewise consider the real course woman ought to take in order to finally find her proper identity—the idiosyncrasy and authenticity that will define women of the future, perhaps many years from now: the "Vindicated Eve."*

# ACKNOWLEDGMENTS

I am extremely grateful to Joan Murphy, Alexander, Vanessa, and above all, Joanna Lopez, who have patiently managed to change my English into a more comprehensive language. Also to my good friend, the poet Juan Liscano, who wrote such beautiful words of introduction.

# FOREWORD

## A PROPHECY IN FAVOR OF WOMEN

This essay, written with feverish pulse by R. E. López-Corvo has not only a psychological groundwork, but also, in its development and projection, represents a cultural and ontic vision of women's place in history.

The author starts by reviewing the Bible's chapter on creation and points out the desire expressed in it to deprive a woman of her capacity to procreate, allying her with the serpent, symbol of the devil, and making her responsible for the expulsion from Paradise. He also points out that God is a male, which would indicate that the episode was devised by men. However—and here begins a very personal inquiry—this conspiracy against women, performed with their own consent has given rise to a complete distortion of their being as well as many of their com-

plexes, frustrations, inhibitions, and—most significantly—
their "castration impulses."

Rich in observations and psychological associations,
this segment is dedicated to what the author calls the
"Delinquent Eve." He distinguishes in Eve three phases:
the first one with a sense of delinquency and adaptation to
the situation, in part protected, in part deprived; the other
confused when she begins her rebellion, due to advances in
biology and psychology; and the future one, utopic, propi-
tiated by electronics and scientific progress, when she will
be replevied. Then, announces R. E. López-Corvo with a
certain humor, matriarchy, which never truly existed before, will arise.

This thesis is schematic but brimming with an erotic
sense (Psyche was in love with Eros and she with him,
eternally), abundant with dazzling intuitions and associations, offering an organic vision of femininity, not obtained
from archetypes or mythology, but from biology and car-
nality itself. Thus, the notion of imprinting appears—a
power more than an action—which charges women with a
decisive gravitational strength over their companions. The
long domestication to which women have been submitted
causes them, however, to fear that power, to fear themselves; and with a masochism fully expressed by one of the
women evoked in these pages, they have accepted the
conspiracy against themselves.

"I started to think," she said, "as I had never done
before, of what exactly it means to be a woman. I thought
of our own bodies, of mine, of my mother's and all the rest.
All are the same, all with a hole. I belong to that immense
herd of perforated beings, at the mercy of invaders. There
is nothing to protect my hole. There is no lid, no blind, no

mouth, no sphincter. It is hidden within soft tissue and does not obey my will; it is not capable of defending itself. In our own language, words referring to this specific part of the female body are ugly, dirty, grotesque or technical." A magnificent and vibrating confession of someone gifted with the power of speech, the "Delinquent Eve" is fully manifested in her words.

In this manner López-Corvo meditates over the sexual organ, male and female, the first obvious, external and immediate; the latter folded back upon itself, interior, hidden, almost imaginary. López-Corvo urges women to be objective within their minds about their own sexuality, which is equal to that of men but covert: ovaries are testicles and the vagina a penis.

An attractive aspect of this essay consists in the will to understand in its biological and corporal functionality, not only sexuality, but also maternity, the most extraordinary gift ever given to women; anality as an impulse and as the counterpart of the uterus; the symbolism of feces; the ancestral feminine inhibition; and man's fear of woman because she carries within her body the power of reproduction. This power provides her with the magic and enchantment of imprinting, "an impression tattooed in the most recondite of the human mind," a force that will irresistibly attract the heterosexual male toward the woman's body, where he once was and from where he emerged, to remain linked afterward during the nursing phase. In this fashion imprinting is born with birth itself. López-Corvo explains that the male undergoes the magnetism of imprinting while the female assumes it, exercises it.

Thus, women have struggled from primitive times to our present days against that carnal, biological, and psychological power that distinguishes them from men, a force that men have associated with fear, characterizing it as obscene or diabolical, an interpretation that women from the patriarchal and *macho* past have submissively accepted.

But women of today are throwing off this burden, equalizing themselves with men in the workplace, and becoming more independent. This liberation, however, induces as a complication, the threat of a conflict that psychoanalysis has emphasized, the well-known complex of penis envy. That is, women are not assuming the power provided to them by imprinting, but instead they imitate men, giving rise to confusion: masculinization of womanhood and feminization of manhood. We are living in an era of bisexuality; the masculinization of women may give them equality, but the cost is often frigidity. López-Corvo's intuition is accurate. And this gift of insight, which might appear as dislocated, is what supplies his essay with a bold fascination.

The readers, however, might feel shaken by the author's theories or perhaps they may differ violently from his views, but it would be impossible to remain indifferent to López-Corvo's amount of asseverations. He is trying to vindicate women's role in history and society, to press them to go beyond their present confusion, to live fully the power of imprinting—wishfully mirrored in men's eyes—and also, to transcend this force, not only through the awareness of their own sexuality, but mainly by reaching, through an abstraction of thinking, their inner intellectual fecundity.

Finally, in order to achieve perfection in his utopia to restitute women, López-Corvo concludes with a meditation about love, exalting and clarifying. *"Love,"* he writes, "means to be aware of the other, as someone different from oneself, as a complete human being who cannot be possessed. . .Love allows us to share, without losing our autonomy or our identity, in complete freedom of expression and in full power of our actions." From a similar perspective, tomorrow's couple will project itself towards a new era where they will age, mutually providing and enriching themselves with affection and spiritual wealth.

Once fulfilled, Eve might overcome her own castrating impulses; or on the contrary, in a vain and an artificial seduction she may become a messiah, and then as part of a couple, she may return to Paradise. This prophecy implies the conversion of God—understanding it as a prototype and not as an archetype—God will be a woman for the well-being of the species. That is, of course, if war, a male invention, and this time a nuclear one, does not finish off our stock.

Juan Liscano
July 1996

# 1    THE COMPLICITY OF EVE

> God created Adam lord of living creatures, but Eve spoiled it
> all.
>
> —Martin Luther

The central theme of this essay consists of an investigation, a true detective inquiry, into a crime perpetrated
during the primeval era of mankind. The idea came to me
after a careful examination of the myth of Genesis, the
ancient history known by us all, and of Adam and Eve, a
common account shared by both Judaism and Christianity, a tale already present in Summerian civilization.

I think that the argument present in the myth of
Adam and Eve renders a violent attack against women:
God, a male, creates a man first, then puts him to sleep in
order to bring the woman into existence, an action that
obviously produces a distorted representation of mater-

nity. Furthermore, Eve thus created, guilty of a satanic seduction, induces an innocent man to sin and in the end drags him away from the forever lost land of Paradise. There is no question that the myth of Genesis instills in women a very negative image of themselves. In the first place, it is decided that God is a male, secondly that "he" created a man first in order to give birth to a woman, an absurd gesture that deprives woman of her biological reality because it is only she who is capable of conception. Finally, a satanic and demonic role is attributed to her, because it is she alone who tempts the innocent Adam and induces him to commit the Original Sin.

Women of other times, heirs of Eve, have never voiced any complaint or word of disagreement about the veracity of such a myth; on the contrary, they have always been, and still are, more religious than men, meekly accepting the double aggression of being both deprived and accused.

We might deduce, following this investigation, that God and Nature have induced in women an inveterate, basic, and transcendental *masochism* that seems to characterize them throughout history for all centuries to come. Women have accepted the disposition of a male God, the loss of their biological right to procreate, and a "delinquent" condition by virtue of their acquiescence to a fatalistic, passive, hormonal, and masochistic role in the phase of which there is no alternative or escape.

Janinne Chasseguet-Smirgel, a well-known French psychoanalyst, has presented her own experience with a group of female patients whose common psychological characteristics consisted in their tendency to associate with men of great risk, pathological criminals who continuously threatened their lives. In her dissertation she raised again the old argument of feminine masochism, by virtue of which women place themselves, in a rather passive and naive fashion, in the hands of calculating and dangerous men who ultimately make them their victims. The thesis was not completely satisfactory, since it presented women as a bunch of fools who lacked the intelligence to avoid being easily coerced into the total control of sadistic criminals.

The answer came to me, I think, sometime later during the analysis of a female patient who presented very similar characteristics to those described in the aforementioned paper. Mary, a thirty-year-old and very attractive but slightly overweight blond of Italian origin, came for consultation because of some depressive features: insomnia, loss of appetite, difficulties in concentrating, and so forth; besides a serious dependency on heroin. At that time she was working as a dancer and singer in a night club in Montreal. Two months before, she had been knifed by the man with whom she had lived for the last six months. After recovering from her injuries, she showed serious signs of depression: irritability, boredom, suicidal rumination, and a diminished desire to live. This was not the first incident of that kind; two years before, another boyfriend who regularly abused her physically was convicted of strangling one of her friends. For some time during her treatment, I supported the thesis, similar to that of Dr. Chasseguet-Smirgel, of an unavoidable masochism as the only explanation for her continuous need for punishment and her compulsion to place herself in life-endangering situations.

A dream, which appeared eight months after treatment began, revealed an unexpected condition, a clue to the understanding of her apparent masochism: *"She was looking at herself in a mirror. Someone from behind, not well-defined, a man perhaps, shot a gun grazing her slightly and breaking the mirror into a thousand pieces."* Her associations to this dream disclosed that the man was not really shooting at her, but at the image of her mother reflected in the mirror; this revealed an unresolved hatred for her mother. As is often found in suicides, it was someone else she wanted to destroy: the desire to make the inner representation of her mother disappear. What the dream really expressed was not only her psychotic confusion between her own body and that of her mother, but also the compulsive need to search for a man capable of criminal aggression, capable of matricide, that is, of killing her mother.

The situation then took on a different perspective: it was not just a simple masochistic desire to seek the company of a man who would hurt her[1], but rather an active and unconscious search for a potential criminal who could be seduced by her and subsequently lend himself, unaware, to perform the crime. Her apparent masochism could then be viewed from a different perspective, not just as it had appeared to other researchers, a genetic trait, the essential and biological condition of an inner need for punishment, but as a psychological defense to avoid seeing herself more as the *offender* than as the *victim*. More acceptable was an imposed and inoculated masochism, a pretense designed to camouflage the desire already established within her unconscious to destroy the inner repre-

---

[1]A condition well portrayed in the well-known movie *Looking for Mr. Goodbar.*

sentation of her mother, which appeared externally as a need for self-punishment and self-destruction. The image reflected in the mirror of her dream represented the phantom of her mother incorporated internally, enclaved and experienced as a foreign body capable of eliciting not only envy, but also a wish to destroy it with rage. The man was nothing but a seduced accomplice, and she an active seducer who narcissistically confused the purpose and place of her crime for self-punishment and convenience.

I then came to the conclusion that perhaps the story of Genesis also entailed a similar conspiracy: that women—true accomplices of the destructive actions men exercise against them—were concealing, in the acceptance of that conspiracy, a different longing, repressed by fear and *not yet revealed*. A question then became imminent: What universal condition is hidden by women within that submissive surrender, as in the case of Mary who concealed her seductive power to feign the state of a masochistic victim? Masochism would not be a final condition, essential and characteristic of a universal psychology of women, but a defense, a screen that veils the presence of a hidden power, a power so great that it may have been concealed through a submissive, unresisting, and ancestral silence by all women for so many years.

It is quite credible that a *masculine* and envious God might have robbed women of both their maternity and their sanctity. But what is incomprehensible is women's apparent dependency, their tamed complicity in establishing a conspiracy against themselves, initiated by a masculine God who deprives them of their gift of procreation and condemns them to be the cause of original sin, and responsible for the loss of earthly Paradise. Such a condition of passive surrender seems to conceal, as in the case of Mary, a *terrible fear* that might hide a *terrible power*: "Tell me what you boast of and I will tell you what you lack," says an old Spanish proverb.

Further inquiry into this biblical "crime" helped me to posit that women indeed shelter a powerful and omnipotent condition, of natural origin, that resides in the deepest core of their biological unconscious—a condition that has provided them with such power and control that just to imagine it, to suspect its existence, has been enough to invert the facts to the point of eliciting in women's general character an opposite attitude, a masochistic façade, behind which they hide a fear of their natural power.

The answer to this confusion emerged from the field of biology. The clue, I thought, lay in well-known experiments carried out by the notable German ethologist, Konrad Lorenz, which he called "Pragung" or "Imprinting." Although experiments of this kind have never been performed with human subjects, no argument exists to contradict the idea that mankind, at one extreme of the natural developmental scale, has also been exposed to the same *fatalistic vicissitudes*; on the contrary, the phenomenon of imprinting has been proven in recent years to be present in all living species, including insects. But I will go into further detail in subsequent chapters, when I shall consider the determining role of imprinting as a power on all women, the fear that such power produces, the temptation to act it out, as well as the guilt induced even by the temptation, and most of all, the relation of all of this complex to the *apparent submission and masochism* often observed in women. This secular battle has defined not only the character of women, but also the true profile of femininity, as well as female behavior and aspirations.

This struggle, it seems to me, also reflects women's need to search for a true identity, a *universal feminine principle*, which will define them as authentic, transparent, without duplicity, exactly as they are in the depth of their hearts.

I have conceived of at least three different phases concerning the historical development of women. The consequence of these phases, we might conjecture, is not culturally equitable due to the many societal differences around the world. However, if we were to take into account our western civilization only, I would say that women, at present, are living between the first phase, which I call the "Delinquent Eve," and the second, the phase of the "Confused Eve." The third phase, yet to come—perhaps many years from now—I call the "Vindicated Eve."

# 2  THE THREE PHASES OF EVE

Nature intended women to be our slaves. . .they are our property; we are not theirs. They belong to us, just as a tree that bears fruit belongs to a gardener. What a mad idea to demand equality for women!. . .women are nothing but machines for producing children.

—Napoleon Bonaparte

Not long ago, surgeons could not rely on all the technical facilities we find available today. Chloroform, for instance, used as an anesthetic, was directly applied over the face using a little mask, a method still known today as "*anesthésie à la reine*" because in the year 1853, John Snow administered it to Queen Victoria during the birth of Prince Leopold, her seventh child. The experiment had been delayed since 1847, when Sir James Simpson of Edinburgh used it for the first time, at which time it was attacked by the Church based on Genesis 3:16, which states that *"in pain shall ye bring forth children"* (italics added). In the end, however, Sir James and his followers were able to impose their criteria, debating that although the Bible was right, it was also true that God put Adam to "sleep" while he removed his rib in order to create Eve. But nothing close to this over-fastidious controversy that I have chosen as an example, or many others witnessed during the course of history, has ever defended the injustice perpetrated against women in this same Genesis: robbing her of her maternity and declaring her in connivance with the demon. Nor did any layman or theologian ever defend women with the same wit as did Sir James, in order to restore their biological right for motherhood or to ease the responsibility attributed to them for the Original Sin.

During the time of the Roman Empire, for instance, women were completely deprived of all rights. The only relevant responsibility I can think of was that of the Vestal Virgins, who were confined for life under the strict surveillance of a high *priest* in order to continuously preserve the flames of the sacred fire, the extinction of which was punished by death. Just as the Vestal priestesses, after the destruction of their temple by Constantine, may have sown the seeds of the creation of convents and nuns, the power of the caesars has provided continuity to the power of the popes. The first important pagans to respond to conversion were the wives and mothers of the Roman aristocracy because they were easily convinced by the fact that, for the first time in history, a real and earthly woman was made chaste and raised to the rank of a goddess: the Virgin Mary, mother of Christ. Other goddesses were just the invention of creative minds and never existed.

Religions, such as Judaism or Islam, also carry in their philosophy that same degrading attitude toward women. I have often thought that *all religions are phallocratic*. The magnitude of this degradation gives room for suspicion of a universal conspiracy *in which both men and women have equally participated*. The paradigm of this woman, submissive and masochistic to the extreme, which has filled so many pages of ancient history, and which unfortunately still determines the culture of many places on earth, I have named "Delinquent Eve."

Meanwhile, years of history have elapsed and women have not allowed themselves to question the position of ignominy they have occupied for so many years: "More noise is made by a falling leaf than by a woman's opinion," says an old Arabian proverb.

Today's woman, eight thousand years more advanced than the woman of Genesis, is trying to find in the idealized image of man the identity she never attained before within herself. Many years of domination have created in women a feeling of inferiority, an image of castration, and an envy for an unobtainable, idealized phallus. The woman of today has tenaciously pursued recognition and equality, reclaiming a lost identity she never demanded before. *It is not, of course, inside man's entrails where she will find her own oneness, her totality, nor in his power, domination, control, or penis; but within herself, in the innermost and mysterious core of her essential being.* "I stopped wearing makeup and shaving my legs, started learning Karate, and changed my politics completely," said feminist Robin Morgan back in the seventies (1970, p. xvi), while more recently, Mona Charen states: "Feminism. . .in return. . .has effectively robbed us of one thing upon which the happiness of most women rests—men" (1984, p. 24).

Much ink has flowed in woman's search for her self-hood, says Simone de Beauvoir. Pamphlets and posters by the thousands have filled squares and parks in continuous demonstrations by "women's liberation" movements in many cities of the world, demanding that men restore an identity they believe them to have purloined. The confusion behind this attempt to compete with men in order to reclaim the realization of such an absence, of this lost identity, has induced me to define this stage in the development of woman as the "Confused Eve."

Many more years must elapse through the long and arduous course of human history before women will be able to take final possession of their own identity, without guilt or confusion, master of themselves, in complete control of the unbelievable power biology has afforded them.

Backlash in women's liberation movements has often been repeated in the past, said Susan Faludi recently:

> *The 'woman movement' of the mid-19th century, launched at the 1848 Seneca Falls women's rights convention and articulated most famously by Elizabeth Cady Stanton and Susan B. Anthony, pressed for suffrage and an array of liberties—education, jobs, marital and property rights, 'voluntary motherhood,' health and dress reforms. But by the end of the century, a cultural counterreaction crushed women's appeal for justice. Women fell back before a barrage of warnings virtually identical to today's,*

*voiced by that era's lineup of Ivy League scholars, religious leaders, medical experts, and press pundits.* [1991, p. 48]

Women's continuous attempts at finding new forms of freedom, of breaking different patterns of oppression from the establishment, have often been repeated during the past in a sort of spiral movement that reiterates its search but fails again. Some time in the future, women will understand that *the mistake dwells not in the purpose, but in its methods.*

Men have never hidden, throughout history and time, the appalling need they have to continuously test their fear of losing their concrete masculinity, by organizing war after war, copiously bloodying the labyrinths of history. Women have never initiated wars, and the tales about beautiful Amazons who ride through the maze of the Brazilian jungle, or the narrow paths of the Hellenic peninsula, are nothing but pure male fantasy more masturbatory than real. Real, of course, is the tour de force continuously displayed by modern powers, led by men—or women imitating them—who display their strength, completely ignoring the rest of us, the spectators who will suffer the consequences of those fearsome metallic rockets, like enormous phalli ejaculating death, brandished with pride in parades celebrating the triumphs of other wars; parades with the sole purpose of impressing and intimidating one another, like adolescents who compare the size of their own masculinity. War has always been, exclusively, a male invention.

Perhaps someone might consider it naive to assume that one day women, once they achieve their lost identity, will be a continuous source of edifying and permanent peace. This imaginary Eve to come, capable of returning mankind to the Lost Paradise, I call the "Vindicated Eve."[1]

The pages to come will attempt to fill the gaps, or to answer the many questions aroused, in relation to the continuous metamorphosis of these three phases of Eve. The "Delinquent Eve," paradigm of Genesis already described, represents a woman who plots with men to construct an infamous slander against herself. How can women's participation in discrediting themselves be understood? What secret covenant has forced her voluntarily to cooperate? Is there, at the bottom of her soul, a restless seed of guilt, the result of some appalling crime, torturing and filling her with remorse? If this were the case, what sort of crime is she guilty of that might explain the source of such masochism? Even more, when women allow themselves to protest, why do they search for the answer in rivalry and comparison with men? Why do women see themselves in "men's mirror," instead of probing inside their own intimacy? Why, in other words, do they succumb to the fascination of external appearance, to the masculine phallus, to perceive themselves castrated, instead of understanding the mystery of their own concealed sexuality?

---

[1]In choosing a name for this particular kind of Eve, I hesitated between "restituted" and "vindicated." Finally I have decided for the latter.

# 3 THE ANTITHESIS AS A DEFENSE

"Tell me what you boast of, and I will tell you what you lack."

—a proverb

In the field of psychology and clinical psychiatry, it is common knowledge that a *symptom* may often be an expression of a hidden conflict diametrically its opposite. A patient who fears being contaminated by imaginary "germs" washes her hands continuously, often lacerating them, while at the same time, dreading contamination by clothes washed at home, she then decides, for at least ten months, not to wash her bedclothes or her own lingerie. Another patient who fears elevators does not seem to mind risking his life by performing air acrobatics while parachute jumping. In psychiatry and psychoanalysis, this paradoxical behavior is known as "reaction formation" because the action performed is reactive—or completely the opposite—to an idea unconsciously repressed, summarized perhaps by the adage I already mentioned: "Tell me what you boast of, and I will tell you what you lack."

What did men, from the time of Genesis, fear so much about women that they changed biology's determinism to its opposite, taking maternity away from them and giving it to men, while at the same time slandering women by associating them with the devil? Nobody can deny a woman her transcendence as a mother. Since the time writing was invented, numberless adjectives have been used to describe her multiple qualities: "Alma Mater," "Mother Country," "Mother Land," "Mother Nature," and so forth. There are also other unconscious motives—psychological and biological—that might help us understand what sort of things men fear so much about women, which have induced them to disarrange the facts. Could it be that men envied a woman's capacity to give birth, to create life, while they, regardless of how much they might have tried, produced none? Obviously women, and not men, were "chosen by the gods" to be the real site of procreation. It is quite feasible that men at the time of Genesis, ignorant as they were, could devise no explanation, and out of envy, decided to deprive women of exactly the quality they so much admired. In ancient Egyptian hieroglyphics, the word *witness* was represented by the male's sexual organs. In Latin, the word *testis* signified both witness and testicles, a root likewise found in the English words *testify and testimony*. We might think of at least two different explanations, nevertheless interrelated: either that man was pondered as being the only one capable of testifying and a woman's credibility was never considered serious enough to qualify her to bear witness, or that *men perceive themselves as mere witnesses to women's capacity to create new life.*[1]

God, and those men who at the beginning of time have coined its gender, might have acted, guided by the power of envy, to invert the importance of women, not unlike the patient who defied his fear of heights, manifested in his apprehension for elevators, by facing the abysmal distances of the sky, or the girl who, in desperation, washed the imaginary germs from her hands, but let them proliferate at the same time in the intimacy of her dirty clothes. But this contentious power men have exercised for centuries against women continued even after science clarified to everyone that men's direct participation was also absolutely necessary to procreation, demanding therefore a further search, a different explanation than the one just provided by the acting out of envious need. There should be, furthermore, an additional cause, something very powerful, emanating from women, fearsome to men as an omnipotent threat, which forces them unconsciously toward the need to compete with women and to revile them.

In any case, I have solely reviewed those ubiquitous tendencies men have displayed toward women without

---

[1]*Couvade* is a French word meaning hatching and it has been used to name a custom, known since ancient times, of the father's taking to his bed at the birth of his child with labor pains, just as his wife did, keeping dietary restrictions or otherwise acting as women in confinement. "In its extreme form," says *Encyclopedia Britannica*, "the mother returns to her work as soon as possible after giving birth, often the same day, and waits on the father; thus the roles of the sexes are reversed."

considering the role exercised by the latter, their apparent masochism, passivity, and free will participation as compromised accomplices in a universal collusion against their own freedom. Men have deprived women of their natural merits, moved by a transcendental and pervasive apprehension—as a "reaction formation"—that has induced them to convert to its opposite the subliminal feeling that women possess, in reality, a great power. But in their deepest core, they fear most that women, by commanding that power of free will, will change the course of history in a fashion men might not desire. Women, on the other hand, due to the same apprehension, behave in a similar manner by helping men in a conspiracy of compliance, by giving them all the power and control, while at the same time appearing not only weak and dependent, but also dangerous as demons capable of inducing iniquity by means of *seduction*.

Mari Cardinal, an Italian writer, has translated those feelings of physical and spiritual flaws, which palpitate strongly in every woman's entrails, with a feminine wit and convincing lore:

> *"I started to think,"* she says *"as I never had before, what being a woman exactly signified. I thought of our own bodies, of mine, of my mother's and all the rest. All are the same, all with a hole. I belong to that immense herd of perforated beings, at the mercy of invaders. There is nothing to protect my hole. There is no lid, no blind, no mouth or nose, no sphincter. It is hidden behind soft smooth tissues, which do not obey my will, and is not capable of defending itself. In our own language, the words used to refer to this specific part of the female body are ugly, vulgar, dirty, grotesque or technical."* [1976, p. 14]

# 4   THE IMPRINTING

An old man once did say
Who could ever be so gay
Of discovering some day
By which strange flaws
By which mysterious laws
Princes are ruled by Kings
And in any occasion it seems
We are dragged more by a bosom
Than twenty large yoked oxen.

—Spanish song

At the beginning of the 1930s, German ethologist Konrad Lorenz, employing contributions from the end of the last century, produced outstanding observations and a hypothesis about the social behavior of birds. While working with the goslings of Canada geese, Lorenz discovered that chicks developed a strong sense of attachment towards any randomly presented object, regardless of its shape or size, if it replaced the mother goose at a given moment of development, even for a short time. He experimented with all sorts of articles, as heterogeneous as a football and an old shoe, and in all cases when the chicks had attained adolescence, they always preferred to follow the football or the old shoe, as if it were their own mother, despite the fact that the contact had been made very early in their life and for only a few hours.

The magnitude of that impression, acquired in such a short period, implied that this phenomenon was more than just a social learning. The memory then, due to its permanent and indelible character, was thought to be a previously unrecognized experience, different from socialization, which Lorenz baptized with the name *"Pragung"* in German, *"Imprinting"* in English.

This behavior implied the existence of a permanent impression that seized these birds for life, forcing them to exhibit the bizarre behavior of following the movement of disparate or ephemeral objects, such as the old shoe, instead of their original mother. Further contributions after Lorenz's initial discoveries have expanded this experiment to many other species, from insects to the most complex mammals, demonstrating how they are always capable of pursuing any arbitrarily selected object that replaced their true mother at a specific phase of their development. Lorenz even experimented with himself as a substitute mother and ended up becoming the parent figure to a variety of birds. An American ornithologist also had, not long ago, the original idea of imprinting ducks to a small remote control airplane, with cameras attached to both wings, in order to film the birds while flying. The experiment was a great success. It was so marvelous to observe their flight in slow motion that I couldn't help but think about poor Leonardo da Vinci's mad struggle to draw flying birds with the naked eye in order to construct his flying machine.

Obviously, it is not possible to carry out experiments of this nature with human beings. However, there should be no room for doubt that we might respond in a manner similar to that of the rest of the animal kingdom. After all, we have known since Darwin's time that human beings are not what we once thought in the past, that is, the unique and favored creatures chosen by the Lord.

If this were the case, that we might respond in a fashion similar to that of other animals, we are then equally attached, males and females, to the memory of our mother's young body design.

> *"Much evidence supports that conclusion and none contradicts it,"* says John Bowlby, a British psychoanalyst. *"We may conclude, therefore,"* he continues, *"that, so far as is at present known, the way in which attachment behavior develops in the human infant and becomes focused on a discriminated figure is sufficiently like the way in which it develops in other mammals, and in birds, for it to be included, legitimately, in its current generic sense. Indeed, to do otherwise would be to create a wholly unwarranted gap between the human race and that of other species."* [1969, p. 223]

*The force exercised by this impression, tattooed within the most profound corner of the human mind, represents the decisive power women exert over their kindred males.* This statement depicts the central theme of this essay, offering a point of view, up until now, not carefully examined, as far as I know—a dimension by which women could be seen in a different perspective. In the chapters to follow, I will use the concept of imprinting to establish the existence of a determining power, empirically sensed and furthermore feared by all women. The threat of such power is so great, I think, that they have preferred to play a secondary role, masochistic if you wish, in order to conceal the apprehension they might experience now and throughout time of acknowledging the determining role they have performed in shaping the historical continuity of mankind. It is not at all surprising, for instance, that artists of both sexes begin their training by painting or sculpting the beautiful bodies of young naked women.

The concept of imprinting helps us to understand why men, in general, display such open inclination towards women's bodies, unless they are, of course, homosexuals. Forced by the invisible thread of imprinting, they move towards women, urged by a fatalistic desire implanted in the innermost core of their infantile souls. How can we then understand that women, on the other hand, react differently, preferring men's bodies to other women's, if they too share the same origins? It is quite logical to expect that women should react in a similar fashion to the forces of determinism.

The phenomenon of "Identification" was originally introduced by Freud. Guided by a similar inquiry—although he knew nothing about imprinting—he discriminated between the notion of identification (to take the place of, to be similar to, etc.) and that of "object choice" (to move toward, to desire the other, etc.), "object" signifying anything or anybody. In other words, the girl or the boy would first take the place of the mother or the father respectively, in order to select someone else from the opposite sex as their "object" of desire, the girls identifying with their mothers and then longing for the man's love, and the contrary with the boys.

The power exercised by imprinting resembles that of the Earth's gravitational force, capable of restraining anything at all from easily breaking away from its field of attraction. In order to facilitate the comprehension of the dynamics present in this parallelism, I would like to first describe the mechanisms by which a child's mind works, and in particular how the transformation takes place according to age and as developmental stages evolve.

At the age of approximately eight months the child's mind resembles a mirror, because it reflects only whatever object is present. Since it lacks memory and is not faithful to the image reflected, the concept of the image reflected will disappear as soon as the object moves out of the line of vision. After eight months, the mind reacts as a picture camera, capturing in the *engrams* (units of memory) the object reflected, allowing the child in this manner to discriminate between the "known" and the "unknown," between the familiar and the strange, giving place to a phenomenon the French psychoanalyst, René Spitz, described as the "anxiety to strangers," a reaction usually observed when babies cry and move away from anyone unfamiliar, and turn towards the mother's arms. At this particular stage, external objects will progressively become captured in the memory, creating the need for a language as a means to provide a name for them, as well as being able to easily recall them. Finally, at a later age, the mind will work as a movie camera, adding movement to mental processes, capable of projecting itself beyond the present and into the future, in the continuous overcoming of time.

During the second stage, when the mind reacts as a camera and traces of the external object are preserved, the child will also acknowledge the presence of the father as someone distinct from the mother. Such awareness helps the child to transcend the mother–child binomial and to move towards the mental triangulation of mother–father–child. The father will slowly exercise his own modeling as a power of attraction to the child, progressively fracturing the symbiotic communion with the mother, neutralizing her gravitational forces and overcoming, with his own active presence, the power of imprinting.

The mother, because of her own biological condition, is usually ready to please the first instinctual needs of her child, while the father at the same time interposes himself between the mother and the child, introducing "law" and prohibition. Such interaction between the mother's pleasing attitude and the power of imprinting, on the one hand, and the appearance of paternal law and the father's power of attraction, on the other, constitute the main psychological drama of the child's first years of life.

The successful achievement of these dynamics could only be guaranteed by a common agreement between both parents. When this is not the case, several pathological complications will appear. Many aspects, cultural and biological, will directly influence the structure of such organization.

In Nordic cultures, for instance, the weather is a determining factor. In order to survive the rigors of winter, even more so in years past when most modern comforts did not exist, family members had to rely on their combined efforts to endure all sorts of dangers, something they could only achieve if they remained united and worked in harmony. Preparations during the summer, the storing of food and heating fuel, was a family affair, and any serious disagreement, rupture, or divorce between the parents could create a life threatening situation for the entire household; after all, the word husband, etymologically speaking, means house-bond.[1] This is why, among many other reasons, Nordic cultures seem to be more strictly religious with less tendency towards infidelity than equatorial ones, where the weather is not a threat. There is a greater menace, obviously more in the past than today, to a family's winter survival, if the husband, responding to the power of imprinting, gives in to sexual attraction for a younger woman and decides to abandon his own family. Sometimes a social defense takes place in the shape of religious preachers, hallucinating fanatics who eulogize the martyrdom of the flesh, and moralize on the sinful danger represented by the demoniacal figure of women.

In equatorial countries, which have only two seasons, with abundant sun and mild, pleasant weather, families are organized under a different logic. Women, usually subdued by their fathers, easily submit, as "Delinquent Eves," to the demands of dictatorial husbands who often need to reaffirm their identity by a *macho* type of behavior.

---

[1] *Husband* is a composed word derived from the Old English *hûs* = house and *band, bon or bonde* = union, meaning "the one who keeps the house united."

Disagreements between the parents, their quarrels and dissociations, the presence of another woman and acted-out unfaithfulness, are not great threats to the survival of the family. There is no need for a special agreement in the face of such bounteous, exuberant, and pleasing ecology. On the contrary, such climatic benevolence results in other complications: the lack of planning for the future, anarchy, irresponsible improvisation, and abandonment, among lower class families, of children born from a long parade of different fathers.[2]

In Latin American culture, the traditional mother is just like another daughter, fearful of her husband as she was of her own father; she supports him when he is present, but betrays him in complicity with their children as soon as he turns his back. This is different in Anglo-Saxon cultures, where there mostly exists a tacit agreement between the parents in order to defy winter's life-threatening demands. In Latin American culture, where the weather is so forgiving, the dissociation and ambivalence of mother and children towards the father create the foundation for corruption and transgression against the law: "pretend to obey when he is present, but disobey when you are not seen."

I would now like to go back to our original inquiry

---

[2]Induced by the fecundity of the Chinese, Mao once said that if the entire Chinese population agreed to jump at the same time, they could overturn the world. I have not been able to avoid the temptation to imagine Mao's assumption as being the only solution to the development of the Third World: that all Chinese join hands and jump together; and thus all the winter inclemencies of the north would become equatorial, and tropical indolence would, out of necessity, give way to industry.

about the problem of identification. How can we explain the fact that women, instead of responding to the law of imprinting by choosing the mother as the place of their desire, prefer the father? This observation holds true up to a point; we often witness that closeness among women is less criticized than closeness among men. Women may sleep together in the same bed, hold hands, or embrace each other in public without being suspected of homosexuality. In public bathrooms men never talk; they don't even look at each other. Once it occurred to me that a good way to sell any product would be to place a sign at eye level in front of each urinal, where men, out of the apprehension of looking at one another, would feel compelled to read it again and again. The situation is probably very different in women's rest rooms, where the communication is more open and relaxed without the threat of homosexual anxiety. It is more common for homosexual men to seek psychiatric help than it is for women. Very often women are more aware of how other women look, how they dress, of their beauty, or the freshness of their youth.

Usually fathers are more of a rival to boys, and more seductive—in the positive sense of the word—towards girls. Such a rivalry between the father and his boy should be balanced enough as to allow the child to also identify and imitate his father, instead of being forced back in fear toward his mother's gravitational symbioses. This situation induced Freud to think that, normally, a girl receives double the amount of care than a boy: she receives it from her own mother who gave birth to her, and from the father, who often is more loving and less competitive towards her than he might be with a boy. This is why women at large are psychologically more sound than men, mostly in their capacity to endure loneliness, even though on the surface it might appear the opposite. Statistics and insurance companies know about this, as well as Greek and Italian movie makers, because there are more widows than widowers. When having to bear the menace of loneliness, isolation, or physical pain, women are more stoic than men. Women tend to outlive their companions more often and much longer than men do.[3]

By means of the process of identification with their fathers, boys slowly take their places, and from there they look at their mothers, and later on, through a symbolical displacement, at other women: someone else who looks like the mother but who is not. The female, on the other hand, keeps her identification with the mother and from there she desires her father's love, and also by symbolical displacement, desires other men. *While men search for their mothers' imprinting displaced on other women, women love in men that which their mothers love*—a tendency only seen superficially, because most therapists know that deep inside the unconscious *everybody, men as well as women, marry their mothers.*

Women do not need to search for the imprinting in other women because it exists already printed within their own being: *They are the imprinting.* They only need to

---

[3]I have always been impressed by women's capacity to free themselves from any trace of shame once they place themselves naked on the delivery table, with their genitalia uncovered, in front of many people completely unknown, while suffering the acute pain of labor, and even more, to be able to repeat the experience several times. I see in the action a great amount of bravery. Someone once said that if men were capable of becoming pregnant, they would only have one baby.

exercise it, to take, by means of identification, the place of their mother. Women seek in men not only the fulfillment of a longing for a better and stronger protection (through men's physical strength or their power of intellect), as their parents once provided them during childhood, they also seek to fulfill their need to love, by contrast, out of curiosity for that which is different or strange, for the orgiastic pleasure of penetration, or because *it is easier to do it than not to do it.*[4]

The male should normally feel sufficient inner security as to have the right to become like his father—not to *be* his father, but to feel *as if* he were the father—and to be able, by symbolical displacement, to love other women different from his mother. The female, in the same fashion, should experience the identical right, in order to take the virtual place of her mother. From there she exercises the power of imprinting to seduce other men, different from her father, by displacement.

Taking the virtual place of the parents is a rather complex phenomenon. I have often observed cases of married women who, after several years and for unknown reasons, have not been able to become pregnant until they decide to adopt a child, and then, very shortly after, are capable of conceiving their own. It seems obvious, in these

---

[4]In relation to this last matter, I recall the observations made by Bertrand Russell about gravitational forces. He once expressed that objects do not fall back to Earth because they are pulled or attracted to it, as Newton stated, but instead, and following the economy principle, because it is "easier" for anything to fall than to keep it suspended in mid air indefinitely, just pure "cosmic laziness." I think that we could explain the libidinal attraction between human beings in a similar way.

cases, that there must be a powerful psychological inhibition of the maternal functions, and that its constraint is
overcome as soon as the mother proves to herself and
learns that she is already a grown woman, capable of
looking after a baby without major complications, and that
she also has a right to reproduce. After all, pregnancy is not
a condition that solely belongs to her mother. I have
observed a similar situation in battered mothers, who
seem to repent after having a baby because they fear
unconscious feelings of guilt, due to the belief that the
child was born out of infantile and incestuous desires
toward their fathers. The baby represents the living expression of the "perpetrated sin," and since the mother
cannot *undo* her deed nor get rid of the problem, she
resorts to "erasing" the child.

In modern times women are enjoying more freedom
every day: an increasing number of young women are
making use of contraceptive pills or devices, living in their
own quarters away from the parental household, are more
open about sexual relations, and so forth. But paradoxically, an increased frequency of frigidity is observed, as if
the greater the freedom, the greater the fear. This new
sexual freedom does not imply necessarily an abolition of
the concomitant apprehension, which prohibits women
from giving themselves fully and obtaining orgasm. Unlike
those who departed traditionally from home, they do not
enjoy the social approval of friends and relatives until after
they have become legally married, giving to their husbands under the accepting view of civil, ecclesiastic, or
parental authority. Only then will her first coitus be
blessed by God, who shall observe them from above as

she successfully gives herself with carnal passion to her husband.[5]

I still remember with great amazement, how when I was only a little boy, a large crowd curiously pushed its way in front of a house at the end of the only street of my home town. The wife, who had just married the night before, was brought back because her husband angrily proclaimed that she was not a virgin. How things have changed in only a few years! Now, the cause of shame has turned completely around. Instead, adolescents purposely search for meaningless relationships in order to lose the infamy of being a virgin, and often pay the price of frigidity.

A phobic patient in analysis came to the conclusion that her fear originated from an infantile fantasy of being penetrated by an enormous penis that would destroy her insides. An early memory helped her to understand: she remembered that when she was around six or seven-years-old, she was playing under the table while her parents were eating dinner, and saw her father's immense penis coming out of his night robe.

During the course of history, men and women have changed the way they face the imprinting. At the end of the last century and the beginning of the present one, women used to totally cover up their bodies. Young men from this time became very excited and incredulous while looking at

---

[5]History accounts that Lucretius advised married women not to move during sexual relations because such demeanor was exclusively a prostitute's domain. He apparently argued that women's movement during coitus had the sole purpose of avoiding pregnancy, and that married women, different from courtesans, had no need of it.

the marvelous spectacle of any young woman who might, in public, carelessly disregard the beauty of her ankle exposed under her long skirt. Such decorum to cover women's bodies induced, paradoxically, a greater desire and curiosity. The need for hidden nakedness, just as one still observes among Muslim women, inspires a sense of condemnation, the feeling that women are dangerous and must hide their bodies in order not to instigate sinful temptations. "It is in women's nature to attempt to corrupt men hereunder, and for this reason wise men should never give in to women's seduction," says the Manu, sacred Indian book of civil and religious institutions (The Laws of Manu, Rule No. 213).

# 5 THE POWER OF WOMEN'S BODIES

To men a man is but mind. Who cares what face he carries or what he wears? But a woman's body *is* the woman.

—Ambrose Bierce

Women, in general, want to be loved for what they are and men for what they accomplish. The first for their looks and charm, the latter for their actions.

—Theodor Reik

Everyone is aware of the importance given to young women's bodies in all printed propaganda, regardless of the product in question. From cosmetics to automobiles, from travel to food, or anything needing to be sold, they usually have nothing to do with women at all. Every minute the senses are inundated with subliminal messages—sometimes not so subliminal—of beautiful young nameless bodies, fully or half naked, for the sole purpose of reaching the primitive and biological core of our unconscious, to disturb the obscure forces of the imprinting, and to induce the consumers to prefer, sometimes without knowing, one kind of automobile instead of another—just as Lorenz's birds, in their ignorance, stocked to the absurdity of a rubber ball.

I believe that the abstract and elusive concept of beauty is probably fatalistically determined by the weight of biology, and that such tropism impels human beings to decide what is beautiful and what is not. "Beauty is in the eye of the beholder" says wisely an old English proverb. I remember an observation made by one of my daughters at a very tender age, when she concluded that one of her classmate's mothers was so poor looking that only the fact that she was her own mother could explain the love and affection her little friend showed towards her. Even more, she wondered how beautiful her own mother was in reality, if she was not capable of defining her looks either. "Love is blind" says the old adage.

The concept of beauty in relation to women is not only different from one culture to another, but it has also changed according to different times in history. We have been able to admire the contrast and great sequence of several works of art: from the chubby Venus de Milo and Samothrace in ancient Greece, to the long and slim Venus of incipient sex left by Memling, Cranach, or Tiziano. Rubens also, inspired perhaps by fat women—after all he married two of them—left behind for eternity a prolific amount of canvas filled with corpulent females, contrasting, no doubt, with the more stylish beauties painted by Modigliani in later times.

In the eyes of men from Western civilizations, it might

be difficult to grasp how Padaung men in Burma experience real libidinal attraction toward their female companions. Padaung women, from the age of adolescence, place metallic rings around their necks, one by one, elongating them to such a point that if they were suddenly removed at the time of adulthood, they could even risk their life by the danger of shock from collapse of the respiratory tract. Perhaps they admired, and wanted to imitate, the giraffe's "elegant" pace. In any case, the phenomenon of imprinting seems to be the only logical explanation. Just like anybody else, these men have perceived, from the depths of their unconscious, the imprinted image of their lengthy ring-necked mothers. This is later displaced to other women of similar looks, who automatically trigger the original phantom, forever stamped in the innermost depth of their humanity.

"Man's worth is for what he does, woman for what she is," said Ortega-y-Gasset, a contemporary Spanish philosopher. Not long ago, a newspaper in Montreal reported a lady—perhaps confused by concepts similar to those expressed in Ortega's maxim—protesting with sorrow the discrimination some females experience as anchorwomen, when television directors attempt to dispense them, once their flesh no longer has the firmness of another time, and does not project the splendor of their youth. "Even the Gods bow at the face of youthful beauty, once they are old," said Plato.

There is no question that beauty is completely relative, and definitely linked to that marvelous image of the young woman we were born from. She may be different from the women of other civilizations, perhaps disliked and rejected by others, but passionately and impetuously wished for by those who particularly identify with such a culture, who search for the symbolic image of their mothers, represented in a woman similar to them.

There is really nothing unusual about this statement. After all, how can one explain, for instance, a tiny male mosquito's capacity, while doing air acrobatics, to grab another tiny female mosquito in a love embrace in order to mate, without any doubt or hesitation and never being confused with another flying insect? Selection takes place with unbelievable exactness.

The never ending beauty contests, continuously denounced by militant feminists as a despicable commercial utilization of women's bodies, corroborate that such competition for the scepter only represents the predominance of one beautiful body over another.

Women are aware of the power of their bodies, and often will use them intelligently to their own benefit. Not long ago, and still today to a certain extent, traditional circles exercised their influence in order to reject any ostentatious use of women's bodies. They usually thought, in these cases, that only prostitutes were allowed to be seductive and provocative by the open use of the physical endowments nature had provided them. "A woman who moves her derrière is either a whore, or is very close to belonging to that group," says an Italian proverb. This prejudice opposes the body to the mind, the physical to the moral, and usually concludes by suggesting that women should not boast about their physical endowments, but should make use only of their intellectual virtues.

A beautiful adolescent, whom I saw in psychoanalytical treatment because of anorexic symptoms, continuously swayed from periods of moderated obesity and careless eating, to periods of emaciation and strict diets. She was the youngest of ten children, and at the time she came for help, she was the only one still living at home with her parents, while the others were already married with their lives completely established. She was struggling alone, searching for her identity and independence, under the weight of her guilt because she felt completely responsible for her aging parents. She continuously moved, ambivalently, between the wish to find her own arrangements in life, and her guilt feelings that her parents would be destroyed if she ever were to leave their side. She showed concern about such dissociation, and also feared the power she was discovering about her unfolding, adolescent, and dazzling body, and most of all, the pleasure she experienced from men's desires. Up to that moment, she had been the youngest girl, the small one, the last, the baby, spoiled, but completely unimportant to all the "powerful" adults who surrounded her. The prerogative she was experiencing from her beauty filled her with apprehension. In her mind, in the fantasies of her internal world, she felt that her body not only belonged to her parents, older brothers and sisters, but was also inhabited by them. She feared offending them if she were to give in to the fascinating temptation of subduing men with her ravishing looks, with the power of her body, and to finally reach that place of "importance" that she never had as the little one. She struggled with her omnipotent body, making it ugly, too fat or too skinny, not being able to remain for too long in between, incapable of displaying the power of imprinting and enjoying the impact of her flourishing beauty. Obesity as well as extreme acne in female adolescents often prove to stem from unconscious fears induced by the

new responses they seem to elicit in men, in their lasciv-
ious gaze and words of desire.

In Latin culture I have often witnessed serious family
crises when children usually reach the age of adolescence
and their sexual secondary characteristics start to appear,
when their pubescent anatomy announces with certitude
the abundance of womanhood soon to come. Sometimes
the family equilibrium succumbs to the apprehension
provoked by the adolescent's more liberal inquiries and
daring actions, consequently threatening the family's traditional morality.

Many feminists, on the other hand, resort to unconscious, or not so unconscious, "attacks" on their bodies
through all sorts of mistreatments (obesity, shabbiness,
cellulitis, carelessness, poor hygiene, etc.), perhaps as an
aggression against men in general, destroying exactly
what they feel men like about them, and paradoxically in
the end, resembling them: "Speaking from my own experience"—said feminist Robin Morgan back in the early
seventies—"which is what we learn to be unashamed of
doing in women's liberation, during the past year I was
fired from my job . . . spent some time in jail, *stopped
wearing makeup and shaving my legs, started learning
karate, and changed my politics completely*" (1970, p.
xvi, italics added).

But if "Confused Eve" assaults her feminine body,
"Delinquent Eve," on the other hand, does not feel in full
possession of it. Whenever she tries to fulfill any of her own
sexual needs, they are experienced with guilt, as if they
were forbidden and sinful desires, and if she ever tries to
satiate them, she fills herself with panic, with religion and
guilt, lowers her self-esteem, and inhibits her will.

# 6 THE "GIRAFFE-WOMAN" OR LATIN AMERICAN "CONFUSED EVE"

Women are animals of short mind and long hair.

—Schopenhauer

One must have loved a woman of genius to comprehend the happiness of loving a fool.

—Talleyrand

In summary, the central thesis presented in this essay states that both men and women are equally attached, by means of invisible biological ties, to the young mother's naked body. This memory strongly gesticulates from the hidden depths of our unconscious, determining without awareness, important aspects of our social and individual behavior. Against this omnipotent impression, an unconscious conspiracy is established, placing men and women on the same level: the first, envious of women's natural powers; the second, fearful of that power, choosing a masochistic outlet that throughout history has belittled her image.

For centuries women have been deprived of their right to know, become aware of, and inquire freely within themselves about the truth of their sexuality. Vienna's social elite, at the end of the last century, was shaken by Freud's great discovery that men could also be victims of hysteria, something completely inconceivable by doctors of that time because the word itself was etymologically derived from hysteria, meaning uterus. How can men, they questioned, suffer from such a disease if he lacks the organ? Hippocrates, who coined the term, explained this psychological ailment as the product of unpredictable "traveling" of the womb inside a woman's abdomen.[1]

Hysteria, we know since the time of Freud, results from the repression of any sexual thought or fantasy considered sinful or unacceptable by traditional moral standards.[2] Obviously, hysteria was more frequent among women because sexual repression was stricter towards them. At the end of last century, hysterectomy, that is, complete removal of the uterus, was a customary recom-

---

[1]Pythagoras, as well as Empedocles, teacher of Hippocrates, held the belief that the uterus was like a different being inhabiting a woman's body, which constantly demanded sex and which became very restless when this was not provided. This resulted in a serious agitation, deemed clinically responsible for the symptomatology of hysteria. In other words, women were just "sex-machines."

[2]At the beginning of this century in Vienna, well-to-do girls were forbidden by their parents to dance a new rhythm, the waltz, because it was the first time in history that male and female bodies came close in order to dance, something that many considered absolutely indecent at that time.

mendation made by doctors as a treatment for hysteria. Such repression of sexuality was an aggressive expression towards the capacity to think freely, a restriction of the spirit, a true epistemophobia[3] that impoverished the mind and structured a state of inner persecution. There was the fear that, at the turn of any free fantasy, an uncontrollable temptation might suddenly spur, bringing to the consciousness an indecent thought that would automatically induce a sinful action. This continuous struggle between the instinctive desires, which usually swarm the primitive and infantile unconscious, and the moral threat to the super-ego of those temptations becoming true constitutes the basis for the Freudian concept of the defense known as *repression*. Whoever represses or hinders the spring of thoughts and the spontaneity of fantasies will also repress, by contamination, all of his or her natural capacity to think. The individual will impoverish mentally in order not to sin, and will shelter within herself the appalling fear of any revealing knowledge.

Only a few years ago, any attempt made by women to increase their freedom of action was considered highly suspicious. Women who drove automobiles, smoked, wore pants, or used make up were absolutely frowned upon by nice, homely ladies. They had to face harsh, tantalizing criticism and were accused of either libertine or lecherous habits. As a matter of fact, the expression of "painted women" still remains tantamount for courtesans. Only prostitutes, having nothing else to lose, could use cosmetics or wear low-neck dresses or short skirts. There

---

[3]From the Greek word *episteme*, which means knowledge, and *phobos* meaning fear.

were, however, several daring women who stood out in the past, but who nevertheless were accused and reviled by history as women of obscure origin or easy virtue, such as Theodora, Empress of Byzantium; Catherine, Empress of Russia; and Cleopatra, Queen of Egypt. At the end of the nineteenth century, there were several women capable of seducing noblemen, kings, and millionaires: Cleo from Merodes, Beautiful Otero, Mata Hari, Mae West, and so on. It seems as if these females became a true outpost for those women who marched after them, real standard-bearers capable of disarticulating traditional systems, probing with their daring behavior and introducing substantial changes in social standards.[4] Other women, less brave than the courtesans and covered by their shadows, followed their path afterwards. *Prostitutes, who risked more simply because they didn't mind so much about preserving their "reputation," opened, without any intention, side trails towards greater freedom. They constituted an essential element in womanhood's history of evolution.*[5]

---

[4]It was Mae West's "caustic tongue, not her sexual behavior," says Susan Faludi "that triggered. . .censorship regularly . . . [she] infuriated the guardians of the nation's morals. William Randolph Hearst called her a menace to the sacred institution of the American family" (1991, p. 114).

[5]Other interesting changes have taken place throughout history in men's social behavior due to the influence of underprivileged groups. Roman nobility, for instance, used a lying down position when eating, different from poor people who were forced by lack of space to sit up, a more practical posture that prevailed afterwards. There was also a law around this time that forbade the cooking or heating of food in taverns, attempting to preserve

In later times, however, Latin women attempted to rid themselves of such a dark heritage by searching for new knowledge that might illuminate their minds, and by refusing, once and for all, to be associated with the well-known statement that Schopenhauer ironically immortalized: "Woman are animals of short mind and long hair."

In Latin America for instance—as well as in many other places around the world—universities have become the central place where many women logically attempt to acquire the necessary illumination for their mind. But the first women graduates were suspicious of a certain ingenuity about mundane matters. They achieved well academically, but flunked in their capacity to mature, to reach a reasonable standard of womanhood. Besides the knowledge they gained, there was also a certain quality of naivety and innocence, up to the point that I always felt that besides such obvious naivety, there was also a certain hidden concession, a masochistic complicity in order to appear innocent to the others, free from the suspicion of being sexually knowledgeable. It seems as if their attempt to acquire new knowledge forced them to sacrifice, in complicity with others—mostly their parents—certain basic instinctive or sexual needs. *They brought their "heads" to the university, but left their bodies at home, on loan to their parents, as a concession in order to keep them calm.* Because of their wish to acquire more knowl-

---

with this imposition the moral principle of dining together with the family. However, single men and travelers felt forced to cook their meals illegally in these places, slowly promoting the idea of what later became the common restaurant.

edge, they allowed their guilty bodies to be retained as prisoners, under the vigilance of those to whom they had given such a power.

This very special condition, where the "sinful" body is sensed as a foreign one, imprisoned and guarded, while the head is brought to the university, so to say, requires a symbolical elongation of the neck, something that makes me imagine these females as "giraffe-women": just university heads, free of any suspicion, attached by a long neck to bodies imprisoned within their own homes, carefully examined by "jailer parents" who continuously insure that the acquisition of new knowledge—in their heads—does not imply in any case, the possibility of sinning. Very often, Latin American women, as Nordics did in the past, sense their bodies as being dwelled in by others, not as their own and sole property, but belonging to their parents and male relatives: uncles and even younger brothers. "In childhood a woman must be subject to her father; in youth, to her husband; when her husband is dead, to her sons. A woman must never be free of subjugation," says the Hindu Code of Manu.

The "giraffe-woman" appears as someone whose intellectual knowledge in different fields contrasts with an inveterated sexual ingenuity, a space where the foreign intervention of the "other," watching from within, takes place—a part of her moral consciousness carefully scrutinizing any sexually suspicious or wicked fantasy.

The "giraffe-woman's" profile could be conceived phenomenologically as a dialectic contradiction between an illuminated mind, filled with new revelations, and at the same time also sheltering an instinctive, dangerous and sinful body that remains incarcerated under the dominion of conservative tradition and morals. From a psychoanalytical point of view, these women's sexuality is usually infantile, lodging the fantasy of possessing childlike sexual organs, fearing penetration that they might be damaged by a penis unconsciously considered out of proportion—a reminiscence of the old fantasy of the little girl observing with astonishment the size of her father's penis.

# 7    THE FREUDIAN WOMAN

The great question that has never been answered, and which I have not yet been able to answer despite my thirty years of research into the feminine soul, is: What does a woman want?

—Sigmund Freud

For Sigmund Freud, the basic or "narcissistic injury" par excellence, was represented by the woman's absence of a penis, something that could be translated as a woman's phallic longing, with the purpose of repairing or fulfilling her biological "fault." In men, on the other hand, the possibility of such an absence is perceived as a threat, as an admonition that his might be lost, a castration fear usually perceived as real by the small boy.

Freudian conception is a phallocentric one, where women represent a sort of emasculated man, filled with an envious desire to possess a phallus that they had lost sometime in their lives, but could recover if circumstances were again favorable. Of course, no man has ever, in natural conditions, lost his penis and no woman has ever managed to make one grow. Such a statement has only a symbolical value.

Women psychoanalysts who follow Freud, such as Karen Horney, Melanie Klein, Helen Deutsch, and Mary Langer, among many, introduced the importance of men's envy towards women's bodies, an argument very similar to the concept of imprinting I have referred to, as well as its relevance in human development.

Not only are women envious of men's genitalia—precisely because it is more obvious, completely external and concrete—but men are envious of the power of women's bodies, as well as their capacity to generate life. This envy, however, induced in men by women's maternity, has remained obstructed because of an intense secular, cultural, and psychological repression imposed upon women by a combination of both men, at large, and women, in the form of "Delinquent Eve," as I have already mentioned.

Pregnancy represents for a woman the maximum expression of a natural narcissism, a feeling of completeness, where she and the fetus nourish each other, while the father, and even the surroundings in general, are psychologically excluded.[1] I have often observed, during psychoa-

---

[1]I have observed, during my psychoanalytical practice, at least four conditions instrumented by people as an attempt to protect themselves from the fear they have about feelings of dependency or need of others and that help them to feel completely "self-sufficient" regardless of whether any of these four conditions

nalytical treatment, how some of my female patients unconsciously experience pregnancy as a form of triumph over their own mothers, that is, believing that they will be much better mothers than their own ever were. Although most women enjoy pregnancy and maternity, I believe that in these cases such competition generates guilt and consequently certain ambivalence, usually reflected in nausea, vomiting, bleeding, threat of abortion, fear of an abnormal baby, and so forth, symbolically meaning either a need for punishment or the desire of freeing themselves from such a threat.

From a phylogenetic, as well as an ontogenetic point of view, men's involvement in the mother-child binomial has a tardy appearance. Primitive men, such as those who lived on Tobriand Island near Australia, had the belief that women became pregnant once they were penetrated by the sea spirit while swimming in the ocean. They did not comprehend the direct participation of men in the act of impregnation, and allowed free sexual relation without any precaution in special houses, and without marriage. At the same time, they exercised very severe prohibitions of other activities, such as eating with strangers. The inclusion of men as a direct participant in gestation has a late historical validation because it required more of a scientific approach than the simple contemplation of a woman giving birth. It demanded the need of a microscopic examination of men's semen, a knowledge of the existence of sperm, and the verification of its participation in the act of fecundation of the ovum. Perhaps this is why men in the

---

should be considered normal or abnormal: a) masturbation, b) drug intoxication, c) obsessive rituals, and d) pregnancy.

past—at the time of Genesis—were much more envious of women than they might be now. At present, they feel more reassured because the information science had provided about their active participation is common knowledge.

Maternity is a concrete and corroborated fact, different from paternity, which required in the past an act of faith, and today the help of scientific testimony. *Pater semper incertus est,* or in the words of Telemacus to Athena in the *Odyssey* (Book I, p. 214):

> *My mother said that he is my father;*
> *but I do not know it,*
> *because a man never knows who begot him.*

In ancient times it was believed that the semen was just a nutritional contribution of men to the fetus's nourishment. Later, when spermatozoa were visualized, a new theory was developed based on the concept of the "homunculus," which stated that the spermatozoid alone developed into a baby, and the women were just a simple recipient who contained and sheltered the children until they reached total maturity—a fantasy already present in Greek mythology, which states that Athena was born out of Zeus' head, and Dionysus was kept alive and delivered by Zeus as well from a furrow in one of his thighs. The great poet, Aeschylus, said by mouth of Apollo in the *Eumenides* (Verse 659–677):

> *Listen, and thou shall own my deeper lore.*
> *To be called mother is no wise to be*
> *Parent, but rather nurse of seed new-sown.*
> *The male begets: she's host to her small guest;*
> *Preserves the plant, except it please God blight it.*

*I'll furnish reasons for my argument.*
*There hath been and there can be fatherhood*
*Though there should be no mother; witness here*
*Olympian Zeus' own self-created child,*
*that grew not in the womb's dark coverture;*
*A branch so goodly never Goddess bore.*

Freud's concept of "penis envy" was the consequence of his observation of women who could be categorized as "Delinquent Eves" because they searched for their own selfhood in men's approval, where envy was overall the necessary outcome of women's need to idealize men. The fact that this idealization, as well as women's envy of men, is still accepted by many as a veracity, does not signify that it will sustain forever the forces of time; truth often changes accordingly with the transformation of history. Freud's conception of femininity was very much related to the form of thinking in fashion at the end of the last century and at the beginning of the present one. In the same vein, it was not possible before Galileo's time to imagine that the earth circled the sun instead of the other way around, because to the neophyte's eye the earth did not move, and the sun moved around: it appeared in the east every morning and declined in the west every night. "But the post-Freudian adhered rigidly to the doctrine of the master," said feminist Susan Lyndon, "and, as in most of his work, what Freud hoped would be taken as a thesis for future study became instead a kind of canon law" (1970, p. 199).

At the end of the last century, experiments in physics brought about the invention of the steam engine based on the accumulation of pressure produced by boiling water and the intelligent manipulation of the vapor through a

series of levers and gears that at the end produced movement. Influenced by these discoveries, Freud thought of
the mind functioning in a similar manner, where the libido
would represent the steam, prompting an instinctive biological source, which might accumulate in the mind and
then search for an outlet. Pathology and normality depended directly on the outcome of this form of equilibrium,
where accumulation implied suffering and expulsion feelings of well-being. Libido, on the other hand, was equivalent to sexual energy and any great accumulation was
translated into a great amount of anxiety, where any outlet
chosen to release such pressure could be translated into
different forms of pathology. Masturbation, for instance,
might be responsible for hypochondriasis or coitus interruptus for another kind of symptomatology. What Freud
was facing at this time, although he changed his vision
later on, was the reality, or the characteristics of the way
women were living at this time: pregnancy was a true
life-threatening situation. There were no forms to avoid it
and both man and wife saw any new gestation with real
panic.

All the anxiety Freud saw in his women patients was
not the consequence of any accumulated libido because of
masturbation or coitus interruptus. It was, instead, the
immediate result of the state of great ignorance about
medicine at the end of the last century in relation to any
form of contraception. Once Freud understood such a
confusion, he could elaborate a new theory about anxiety
more attuned with psychic reality, but I will not continue
in this elaboration in order to avoid further complications.
In any case, all theories always appear within a particular

context, and cannot avoid experimenting with influences from other branches of science.

Freud had the intuition, as well as an incredible capacity of observation, that allowed him to become aware that anatomical differences between boys and girls had a determining consequence in mental development, giving shape to the concept of castration anxiety, a very important formulation in the theory of psychoanalysis. Women envy a man's penis because they have failed in their capacity to conceive the hidden complexity of their own mysterious sexuality, a form of thinking that I have categorized as "Delinquent" and "Confused Eve." Once women resolve the puzzle of their concealed sexuality by means of abstract thinking and the power of imagination, penis envy and castration anxiety might ease and finally disappear, just as in the past men's envy of pregnancy and childbirth dissipated once science delivered the existence of spermatozoa as well as their participation in gestation.

In the next three chapters, I would like to review some aspects I consider crucial because they represent a series of natural obstacles that interfere with the psychological development of all women. In the first place, I will contemplate a disarray that very often exists in the mind of every little girl, as well as many grown-up women. I am alluding to the confusion between vaginal and anal functions or the "cloaca theory," because "cloaca" is the name given to certain animals in which the two functions are normally combined. In the second place, I will consider the relationship between penis envy and anal development as two important issues, and in chapter eleven, I will refer to the need, common among "Delinquent Eves," to resort to magic as an outlet for their restrictions, hopelessness and desperation. Chapter twelve, on the other hand, will evaluate the difference between magic and true creativity, as seen in the philosophical concept of alchemy.

# 8     THE CLOACA THEORY

"What makes learning to masturbate so difficult late in life is that we have been raised to believe that the area between our legs is untouchable, dirty."

—Nancy Friday

To assure himself of his sexual identity, man, contrary to woman, only needs to look at the tangible evidence of his external genitals, right in front of his eyes, which define him. In woman, the genitalia are hidden and unseen, lost in the interior of the anatomy. Woman can only be conscious of her genitals through abstract thinking and as a consequence of previous knowledge, which permits her to recreate and envision in her mind organs that at sight she seems to be lacking: to herself and others there appears to be more of an *absence* than a *presence*.

It is feasible that a woman—above all a little girl—may envy the concreteness of a man's genitals, easily visible and capable also of affording orgastic pleasure. Woman's envy for the male penis is undoubtedly an authentic sentiment, but conditioned by a multitude of factors that define and determine the depths of such emotions.

Something exaggerates in a woman, in the "Delinquent Eve," the sense of deficiency, of absence, in the presence of the male phallus: a damaging invalidity in the face of the impossibility on her part to construct in her imagination the presence of her hidden genitals. Something more than its tangibility makes the phallus an object of envy. In the first place, it is difficult for her to desexualize her thoughts, to feel that she has the absolute right to her own body and all the pleasure she can derive from its stimulation, of being thus able to fantasize freely and without self-imposed restrictions, in order to structure clearly and internally the absolute certainty of the presence of her genitalia. Perhaps as an exaggeration of what I am trying to say, I recall the case of a psychotic patient who sexualized intensely all mental activity, to the point of abandoning his engineering studies because for him all theoretical instruction unfailingly became connected with activities of another description, generally with relations of a genital nature. In this way, for example, the theories of acceleration of bodies, pendular motion, attraction of masses, and so on, became sexually charged.

There is nothing new in the idea that the sexualization of deeds and thoughts obstructs good intellectual development. Fifty years ago, schools were not mixed, girls of good families received academic instruction in the security of their homes, in the charge of special tutors, because attendance at regular schools was forbidden by their parents. In Latin American countries, professions that could be considered as "sexualized" by their own nature, such as medicine, nursing, or social work, were prohibited to "good girls," who tended to prefer such studies as architecture, pharmacy, or psychology. The portrait of the "whore-nun" many women experience within is closely related to this dichotomy that parents exercise on their daughters, between seduction and prohibition. The other day, a mother came to the consulting office complaining bitterly about her beautiful twenty-four-year-old daughter, whom she had previously encouraged to perform in television commercials, but who had dared to show her "belly button" while advertising a bikini, "just like a whore."

The power of imprinting also has a definite repercussion on the intellectual future of a woman. The magnitude of the narcissistic gratification she derives from the beauty and enchantment of her body makes it unnecessary to seek fulfillment and satisfaction in developing the potential of her mind. In an old French movie, a character, complaining of the aggressiveness and competitiveness of present day women, exalts in his desire to make love with a woman he describes as "sex in its pure state, with no intellectual contamination." "A woman thinks with her vagina," says an old aphorism.

To let the imagination run wild always carries the danger that hidden temptations, repressed in a woman's mind, might emerge; that restraints could be broken and that primitive and anarchic sexual desires may burst forth and uncontrollably flood the consciousness; that moral limits will be inverted and libertinism will prevail. This type of restriction is more typical of women from the past, of "Delinquent Eves," who felt socially obliged to repress their sexuality, or face the danger of being accused of demonic inclinations.[1] Thus, a dialectical contradiction arises between an instinctive sexuality with an anatomically hidden genitalia that requires imagination and abstraction in order to make its presence felt, on one hand, and the conflict of traditional social repression that limits thought and makes abstraction impossible, on the other. By virtue of such a paradox, it would be difficult for a woman to arrive at a sexual equivalent and be able to compete with the tangible and obvious phallus of men, who, in addition, not only have little fear of sexual thoughts, but cultivate them as a result of macho cultural pressure.

Therefore in the heart of the "Delinquent Eve," a fatal trap creates turmoil: she is afraid to think for fear of sinning, but at the same time, not being able to achieve an inner and abstract perception, she is unable to conceive of the "presence" of her hidden sexuality. The unspoken norms of our culture stipulate that when a woman exercises her freedom she is a libertine, but when a man does not exercise his own, he places his masculinity in question.

There exists, as well, other circumstances equally important, which contribute to the obstruction of a full understanding of women's sexual identity. In addition to the type of intellectual interference mentioned, biology conspires via a confusion that obscures comprehension of

---

[1]K. Schwartz, in his book *The Male Member*, states that the present custom of kissing the foot of the Pope arose in the eighth century, after a Pope (unnamed in the book) decided to cut off his hand when a woman grasped it with exaggerated force to kiss it (Schwartz 1985, p. 37).

the true end of many somatic functions. The vagina, for example, reveals at a rather late date its real participation in procreation and orgasm.

At the beginning, this organ merely performs an excretory function, inasmuch as, to the eyes of a little girl, it produces only urine, a function not altered by the masturbatory activity normally practiced at this age, which is usually clitoral. As a result of the outburst of puberty, the excretory function of the vagina is confirmed once it becomes the outlet of menstrual blood, considered in itself something shameful and dirty. Thus, the vagina represents for the pubescent girl the organ through which undesirable secretions emerge: urine, a waste substance, and menstrual blood, which flows like a silent cry from the uterus preparing itself for conception, that appears to bleed in protest to the void of fertilization.

For the girl, the vagina, rather than the site of sexual pleasure it will be later in life, is instead an excretory opening for undesirable substances of which the organism wishes to free itself. The origin of the pubescent concept of the vaginal role as shameful is related to the anal mechanism, in that both are organs through which any living person frees themselves of waste material. The anatomical proximity of the two apertures also contributes to the possibility of contamination and confusion. This was the reason why Freud, in 1909, proposed the "Cloaca Theory," according to which, as in many inferior organisms, the anus and the vagina appear to be merged in the depths of the feminine unconscious, as though they were anatomically the same organ. It is frequently observed that a menstruating woman resists with a sense of shame the amorous advances of her companion, even more so if she practices a religion that prohibits sexual relations during menstruation.

In the practice of psychoanalysis, we observe the shame experienced by a woman in relation to her menstrual cycles. It originates, in part, from a confusion between the *vaginal* and *anal* activities. There is no justification for such a rejection of the menstrual blood that is nourishment for a future baby. It is perceived instead as undesirable and dirty, a contamination even for the coitus. The discovery on the part of the woman of the orgastic purpose of the vagina does not manage to neutralize such primitive and infantile convictions, which remain present, although hidden and repressed. They are determining factors in female psychology and are frequently inclined to arouse a sense of worthlessness and ignominy. "Woman cannot really know how she is formed, as she cannot satisfy her desire for observation, knowledge and certainty. On the other hand it is easy for the man; he cannot escape his own subjectivity," says Elizabeth Leonelly (1984, p. 34).

The Castration Complex, a central theme in Freudian theory, would also appear to depend on this perception of anal contamination and sense of worthlessness in the feminine mind, and not only a product of the absence of an external phallus. This idea of the participation of anality within the castration complex is not alien to the classical psychoanalysis of Freud, who proposed the concept of "anal castration."

# 9 THE BASIC INJURY

Intimacy is transparent.

Human beings are animals afflicted with consciousness.
—Miguel de Unamuno

The most important characteristics of anality are the feelings of shame and disgust. Humans are fatalistically condemned to exist sheltering within the frame of their own biology an activity that on one hand, is indispensable for their existence, but, on the other, constitutes a place of greatest abomination. Although the anal function is common among all living species, humans differentiate because of their feeling of shame and disgust towards their functions of excretion, which is completely absent in the rest of the animal kingdom.

From a phylogenetic point of view, we could think that the point of "hominization," mentioned by Teilhard de Chardin as the moment in evolution when the anthro-poids (monkeys) changed into humans, must have been determined, among many other things, by a feeling of *shame*, which animals obviously do not experience. Man is an animal afflicted with consciousness, implied Miguel de Unamuno. Ortega-y-Gasset, on the other hand, proposed to visit a zoo in order to watch the monkeys and observe how their main concern is with the "Other", and with the people around them—in Latin, the "*alter*." They live continuously *altered* and at the same time, find it impos-sible to become self-absorbed. They cannot, in other words, free themselves from the determining weight of being altered by the Other's presence. The monkeys mimic and replicate other people's behavior without identifying with it because the action remains foreign and is not at all imbibed. Contrary to animals, men are capable of assimi-lating whatever they imitate or learn, to rob and change it into something of their own, to impregnate it with their own intimacy. It is perhaps this capacity of assimilation that determines the advent of consciousness, of moral consciousness, and shame as a consequence. Whatever determines the capacity that human beings have to take over other people's behavior as if it were really theirs might be what also instigates feelings of shame, disgust, and guilt: the monkey only imitates the Other, the one who is really responsible for the action, but men, by identifying completely with the Other, feel that they have done it; they feel responsible.

It is possible to imagine the emergence, in the mind of primitive men, of a feeling of shame in relation to a greater awareness of anality, inducing in them the need to find a hidden place where to deposit their disgusting excrements, far away from the critical looks of their congeners. *The invention of the latrine constituted a transcendental moment in the evolution of mankind, because it might have contributed to the first attempt towards socialization, and to the creation of different social castes, dividing and separating within the primitive group, between the elite—whose sophistication brought them to hide their anality—and those considered more vulgar, ordinary, and socially inferior because they publicly shared their excretory functions.* The toilet then originated as a necessary location where men could hide those functions that were common in the rest of the animals by which they were normally surrounded. It became a place of evolutional sophistication where men attempted to free themselves of their shameful and vulgar genealogy. A great amount of mankind's suffering stems from this dissociation between what men might consider beautiful and sublime in their biology, and the determining concreteness of the anus, which is normally confused with the most despicable of all activities in all living species: defecation. I have observed during the psychoanalytic treatment of some patients—mainly women—the presence of an unconscious fantasy that induces them to believe in the existence of another type of people. They are completely idealized according to the patient's needs (money, beauty, skin color, size, intellectual capacities, etc.), and who are free from any unpleasant nuisance, weakness, or mistakes, including defecation; some kind of "assless" creatures, different of course, from themselves who are the only ones specifically condemned and symbolically forced by nature to earthly needs.

Even more, the bathroom, to this very moment, represents a "transparent intimacy," because whatever we perform there daily is well known to everybody, completely familiar and ordinary. In this way, anality, as well as the feeling of shame and disgust that goes with it, contributed without question to the development in men of that very high and abstract sentiment of *intimacy*.

Whatever happens in phylogeny is also repeated in ontogeny; or in other words, whatever happens in the history of the species is also repeated in the development of a single man. No child is capable of understanding the logic behind toilet training because, just like animals or primitive men, children do not shelter any disposition of disgust or shame towards their own excretory functions. On the contrary, the feces has a unique symbolical meaning for babies: it is the first "product" coming from their own bodies, generated by them, and to which all adults seem to dedicate and express an immense interest, usually begging or threatening the children to either provide it or to hold it in. It is quite rational to suppose that the child will understand this concern as a sign that such a "product" is of great value, if not vital to those adults around them. This sentiment sheltered by the baby might increase or diminish according to the attitude displayed, usually having, as a consequence, a pathological increment of the feeling of omnipotence already existing in all children. Omnipotence is the most important psychological defense children display in order to protect themselves from an unknown and threatening environment mostly run by grown-ups—strong and powerful people—who threaten their own biological fragility. Children are continuously searching for any situation in which they can make use of their omnipotence in order to hide their feebleness, while at the same time lodging the fantasy that they are really in control.[1]

The greatest surprise, however, takes place when the baby, deciding to give in to the parents' continuous demands, finally chooses to offer a "gift," and encouraged by the many cheers, applause, and pampering, at last deposits the feces in the right place: the toilet. But then, to the child's disbelief and astonishment, they flush it down! Such a circumstance must imply to the child a situation of complete confusion, abasement, and humiliation, a condition, I believe, to be as shocking as the trauma of birth. The existential paradox that destiny and human need for socialization has thrown upon all children, the terrible

---

[1]The "impotence" normally experienced by all babies, in contrast with the greater physical power of adults, conditions in the former a feeling of "omnipotence" as a compensation and a psychological defense against their feebleness. It changes reality into its opposite, as an evolutionary delusion that mentally helps the babies neutralize the apparent threat. This phenomenon can be frequently observed, for instance, in the endless game everybody has witnessed, loved by small babies and impossible to sustain by any adult, where the child—usually inside the crib— repeatedly drops an object on the floor in order for the adult to pick it up and return it to the baby, who perpetually will drop it again and again. Later on, when the child is able to walk, this same game becomes a tragedy, because instead of throwing the object from the crib it might be done from the balcony. The child then bitterly cries, looking down and pointing at the toy that does not come back, until the adult fetches it and returns it. Once the toy is handed back, the child will run again to the balcony to let it go as before and to cry again at the absurdity of this action. In their minds children are completely certain that the toy is not brought back by the adult, but that they have done it themselves with the use of their absolute omnipotent power.

discrepancy between adults' persistent interest in the need to defecate in the right place (plus the feeling of pride children experience when they accomplish a task so highly demanded), and the great indolence with which they make the "gift" disappear, constitute I believe, *the greatest narcissistic wound, or essential injury to their pride, that all children must endure.* This hypothesis, however, differs from the classical psychoanalytical supposition that establishes that the main narcissistic injury stems from the discovery, by boys, that girls have no penis, and that they could lose theirs, if their expected behavior does not conform with their parents demands. I think, as I have stated, that the terrible frustration that all children must experience, boys and girls, over the true meaning of feces, represents in their developmental history a transcendental and painful discovery, which reality forces upon us: the beginning of an appalling distrust and suspiciousness that feces are not gold but just feces. In clinical psychiatry, we are familiar with depressed patients who believe that all they "produce" is feces, where the manic cases believe the opposite, that what they "produce" is pure gold.

As I just stated, socialization demands, among many other things, that all human beings properly accomplish a complete anal education or toilet training. We all know that youngsters cannot attend school if they have not achieved a voluntary domination of their sphincters, and that adults, as well, will not be accepted publicly if they do not know how to behave properly: avoiding the use of bad words, picking their nose, having bad breath, or losing their temper. Sphincter control, however, is not just a plain biological function. There are also at least two imaginary *mental sphincters.*[2] One is located deep inside the self, between that which is unconscious and conscious, regulating our inner communication with ourselves. It is a sort of moral sphincter that operates accordingly with our own ethical standard, only allowing the passage of the acceptable, while forbidding or "repressing"—to use a more psychoanalytical expression—the undesirable. It is this mental internal sphincter that determines the origins of all mental pathology, because if it squeezes too hard, it might induce the appearance of a hidden or "repressed" personality, a dissociation or splitting of self-hood, capable of inducing confusion as well as great suffering and anxiety. The other mental sphincter is located between the inner self and the outside, controlling and regulating communication as an expression of prudence and cautiousness. Socialization depends mostly on the good use of this function, which exercises such a paradox of maximum freedom towards the inside, knowing it all to the point of absurdity, while at the same time, being careful enough in

[2]The word sphynx originates from the Greek, signifying sphincter, which means "to squeeze," perhaps because the Sphynx was trying to squeeze the truth from its victims. The Sphynx was a mythological monster, half woman and half lion, which demanded from any traveler the solution to its riddle: "Who is the animal that walks on four legs in the morning, two in the afternoon and three by night?" The answer was the growing or evolving man, who crawls as a baby, walks on two legs when mature and then needs to use a cane in his old age. Once Oedipus guessed the answer, the Sphynx in despair committed suicide by jumping from a cliff. I think that the symbolical meaning of this myth could imply that men, as they evolve, must face the facts of life, the absolute authenticity regardless of its cost, instead of lying to themselves by "squeezing" out the truth because of fear.

what is shared with the outside. An old Arab adage states: "When my words are inside my mouth they belong to me; once they go out, I belong to them."

No other function in human beings suffers as much repression as the anal activity, despite the danger, as we will see later on, of sacrificing a great portion of human creativity. In the next chapter, I will try to discriminate between anal and vaginal functions, a concept extremely important for women to establish if they wish to achieve a full control of their own sexuality, a feeling of self-sufficiency, and a good level of self-esteem.

# 10    Anal Space, Uterine Space

How can he be clean that is born of a woman?

—Job, 4:4

A great amount of sexual repression among women derives from the attitude displayed by their mothers. I say mothers more than fathers for two reasons: in the first place, the natural closeness of the mother at that age secures a more regular supervision than by the father. In the second place, mothers identify more with their daughters, and as a consequence, they feel they have the right to exercise a greater control. According to the orientation that the mother chooses, she introduces two different possibilities: either differentiation, freedom, independence, high self-esteem, and creativity, or, on the contrary, control, domination, dependency, fear, insecurity, and symbiosis. She will manufacture within the depth of the unconscious, the prospect of two directions, of two different worlds: one dominated by reality, the other by fantasy. I am not saying by this that fantasy is something we ought to disregard as bad and dangerous. What I am stressing is that fantasy can be used to change reality, if that is what we want, instead of remaining forever entangled in a desire or dream that we have confused with reality, and persisting within that fantasy, thinking that it is, in fact, reality. I am aware that I am referring to extremes here; however, we all know that life is not just black and white, that there is a large scale of grays in between. Fantasies are just dreams, where reality is action. A world dominated mostly by daydreaming, for instance, is a world of paralysis, ruled by the unconscious, but a powerful necessity to remain forever attached to our mother's desire, where growing, initiative, decision-making, action proneness, and wish-fulfillment are nothing but obscene intentions, dangerous, and silently forbidden.

Humans, in general, evolve trapped by the dialectic of these two opposite worlds, unanimous and interconnected, like the two sides of a coin. On one side, there is the constraining dimension that restricts us to a particular space and time: *to be here, now*. On the other side, there is a disarticulated world, empty of time and space, that is only useful for building dreams and fantasies: *to be anywhere, anytime*. There is an equilibrium between both, and even while awake, for instance, a part of our brain continues dreaming: it is enough to close our eyes for a moment to see an infinite number of images against the darkness, moving and wiggling with a will of their own. By the same token, when these strange images take hold of our minds while sleeping, and subsequently weave our dreams, one part of the brain remains alert, patrolling, in order to keep us aware that we are just dreaming; we will awaken, for instance, at a given hour or when hearing an unfamiliar noise. Psychosis or madness takes place any time that both worlds intermingle and get confused, be it temporary or during a chronic state of mind. Psychotic patients, for instance, might be able to dream about their wakefulness, because a chemical disturbance forces them to lose their stronghold on reality and to submerge power-less inside a disarticulated world of dreams. Nightmares, on the other hand, take place when the patrolling part of our brain during sleep falls asleep itself and the dream material gets confused with reality. We then feel, regard-less of the content of the dream, that whatever we might be dreaming about is absolutely true: at that particular mo-ment, anxiety appears and we are awakened.

Dreaming reveals to our consciousness a world of unconnected absurdities, completely free of time, space, and symbolical logic, different from the restriction of ex-ternal reality. Within the unconscious everything is possi-ble, just like the sidereal and astronomic world, empty of cardinal points where up is down and down is up. During childhood, when the unconscious is just on the surface, fantasies play a determining role in the form in which children apprehend the universe that surrounds them. For instance, they might imagine that mothers become preg-nant through the mouth, by the food they consume, or think that childbirth is performed via the anus, a connec-tion that convinced Freud of the unconscious relation-ship—in children's thinking—between babies and feces.

As I have already stated in the previous chapters, the pressure exercised by mechanisms of socialization induces the mother to place great emphasis on the process of toilet training, causing the child to establish a direct connection between the mother and the feces, and to make of defecation a means of omnipotent control in order to subdue the powerful mother. The greater the emphasis the mother assigns to the child's fecal production, the greater the omnipotence and the idealization of feces.

Regardless of the anatomical nearness of the anus and the vagina, together with the production of feces by the first and children by the latter, as well as a developmental confusion within the depth of the unconscious, it is obvious that their functions are quite antithetical.

Once the egg has been fecundated by the spermatozoid, life will grip, with an extraordinary obstinacy, to the depth of a mother's entrails, changing continuously until the fetus takes shape inside the uterus, and is then born, inexorably, at the end of nine months. This summarized sequence of the complex processes of fecundation and of maternity adjusts itself to such a fatalistic chronometry *that we might conclude that the uterus is without any doubt a harbinger of time.* But the natural, symbiotic and internal fusion between the mother and the baby is fractured during childbirth, giving place to a new human being, different and separated, who will grow to become an independent individual. By making an external creature from the internal fetus and by creating a separation between both—mother and child, you and I, internal and external—*the uterus is also a forerunner of space.*

Maternal love (as well as paternal) is tragic, said Erick Fromm, because the more the mother loves her children, the more she wishes for them to leave and to separate; while love between woman and man is the opposite: the more they love each other, the more they wish to remain together. Women who have properly identified with their uterine function induce growth and differentiation, in spite of the implicit tragedy.

Anal function, on the other hand, has a completely different phenomenology, because the anus not only produces feces instead of children, but is also capable of reverting its purpose and on volition, retains its product, denying—unlike the uterus—the possibility of *time* or *space* formation. Intense needs for "controlling" and "retaining" are specific character traits that we know, since Freud, as characteristics of anal processes, and constitute what we call in psychopathology, an "anal retentive personality."

When a mother faces the pain produced by the separation of her children, she can, as an unconscious defense, make use of the mechanisms of psychological retention, of overprotection, in order to induce dependency among them and to stop the mental process of differentiation. Normally, parents deal with these needs and at the end are able to give in to their children's demands. In pathological cases, however, mechanisms of retention are extended to the extreme, creating difficult situations where separation becomes so threatening that it could even provoke psychosis. Mothers who are well identified with their maternal role will produce, symbolically, "uterine" babies, while mothers with a poor feminine identity, fearful and insecure, will symbolically give birth to "anal" babies.[1]

---

[1]It is my belief, from the psychoanalytical treatment of pregnant women, that most of the symptomatology observed during this period (nausea, vomiting, headache, etc.) corresponds to a

Within the unconscious core of every neurosis, there
is always a common denominator: a confusion of both time
and space. In relation to time, for instance, past incidents
are eternal, always felt as if they were continuously
present: what happened before is still taking place now.
Space confusion, on the other hand, implies that internal
feelings are projected outside and experienced as if they
really belong to others, or on the contrary, other persons
thoughts or affects are experienced as their own, which is
the essence of paranoia.

Although I may be risking the danger of reductionism,
I think that, in general, healthy and normal behavior is
more related to a "uterine" type of organization, while
pathological conduct might originate more from an anal
type of fixation. While symbiosis is more connected to a
sort of retaining, controlling, or anal interaction, independence is associated with releasing, emancipation, and
liberation; *after all, if the uterus expels, the anus
squeezes.*

Obviously, it is easier for a mother to identify with her
daughters because, after all, both bodies are alike: they are
a well-known and familiar terrain. At the same time, she
will be inclined to move away from her sons, who are
experienced as different and strange, as if they were from

feeling of insecurity and fear about performing their maternal
role. There is the unconscious belief that maternity only belongs
to their mothers, that nobody else has the right to get pregnant
and to have babies. On the other hand, there is the unconscious
desire to compete with their own mothers and to show them, out
of revenge, how to raise a baby with love, how a "good maternal
job" should be properly performed, instead of the "lousy job"
they feel their mothers did with them.

"another race," even though boys are born from the same womb. This unconscious selection helps boys to break away from their mother's gravitational attraction, and to move towards identification with the father. This same selection can increase the dependence of girls, and when this is exaggerated, may foster in them a psychological symbiosis. The *power of imprinting* is passed on right then to the daughters, while the boys witness it from a distance, like their fathers, experiencing the longing for something they want and need, but which is only perceived outside of them. This easier and more natural tendency of mothers to identify with their daughters, to sense their bodies as if they were their own jurisdiction, provides them with a license to intervene and to control the girl's intimacy, much more than they might do with their sons. The greater the repression against sexuality, the greater the impossibility of searching and exploring freely, of being masters of their own bodies and desires. In other words, masturbation for young girls is completely forbidden. Almost every woman that I have seen as a patient shows, as the core of her main conflict, a great ambivalence between her secret masturbation on one hand, and strong feelings of guilt and remorse on the other. Masturbation becomes an area, or better a bastion, so well sheltered and defended that women experience it as the real center of their intimacy, without ever thinking how ordinary and common it is. After all, it appears that most of the women share the same principles and the same fears. When women get together, for instance, they might feel free to talk about their sexual experiences with men, how they perform in bed, the size of their penises, and so on, but very seldom will they utter a word about their masturbatory fantasies.

Furthermore, I found a certain kind of defense in women, more than in men (or perhaps of a different quality than in men), which reminds me of lizards that break off their wiggling tails in the face of any threat, in order to distract their enemies and then escape. Whenever I see a woman who seems ready to agree with whatever she feels the other person says or wants, I feel very suspicious that behind this pleasing attitude, there is the fear about having her hidden masturbatory sexual fantasies discovered.

The identification of mothers with their daughters often results in the increment of powerful symbiotic ties between both, where the daughters feel smothered by the mother's needs, often paralyzed and guilty about any attempt towards freedom, self-sufficiency, autonomy, or independence. There is often a silent, but certain, metamorphosis in women, from the category of young and rebellious, to the position of motherhood, when many principles that were then defended become inexorably changed into more traditional and conservative standards. Several actions that were previously bitterly criticized in their own parents are now being exercised towards their children—mostly their daughters—as if the real argument of this change is just a memory problem, because any complaints and promises they might have previously defended are now completely forgotten.

# 11  THE POWER OF MAGIC

All witchcraft comes from carnal lust, which is in women insatiable.

—Kramer and Sprenger, Inquisitors
(*Malleus Maleficarum*, c.1486)

It appears interesting to observe how the necessity to understand the world by means of magic induces men at large to search in ancient religious books for an answer to modern needs and queries, as if time had not elapsed. I still remember, when several years ago, I decided to revive my own childhood experiences of "house magic" while playing with my oldest son of five or six years of age, who, very impressed, jumped out of joy whenever I performed a new trick. However, when I decided at one point to reveal to him the true nature of the game, I was astounded to find my son throwing himself on the floor, crying and dejected. It took a few times before I could understand that he was not interested, whatsoever, in understanding the hidden mechanism of tricks, or being taught anything about prestidigitation. His main enjoyment consisted in thinking that his father had the unbelievable power to make things appear and disappear, that he was mighty and omnipotent. He was terrified about the threat of finding out that everything could have been just a lie.

The feeling of this child is not completely unfamiliar among the rest of human beings. As a resource, when we have to meet everyday anxieties and experience impotence in the face of life's continuous demands, the need for a special power which might allow us to have access to Nature's apathy or to God's indifference, becomes very tempting. It is not possible to understand otherwise why such immense hunger for religion brings about a dangerous paradox, where fanatics in search of immortality bring death instead: the never ending wars between Catholics and Protestants in Ireland or between Arabs and Jews in the Middle East. It seems that the fear induced by men's impotence, fragility, or finiteness forces them to lose the only thing that they possess, at least temporarily: their own lives. Caracas, for instance, is a city with a high rate of delinquency and a great discrepancy between the indigent and high class dwellers living vis-à-vis, as in many other Latin American metropoles. There are at least two situations in which rich people really feel the need for help from the poor, up to the point that they are willing to risk their own lives—and they usually do—when venturing at forbidding hours inside the red zones of the city (poor and dangerous areas) in order to get either illegal *drugs* or *magic* by visiting the pushers or fashionable witches and sorcerers. It is also common to read in major newspapers long letters or poems in the form of obituaries, addressed to kin long time deceased, as if there were, in the mind of the relative, the fantasy that the defunct gets out of the tomb every morning in order to read the newspaper.

Women at large have a greater inclination towards magic, reflected in the ancestral tendency towards passivity, dependency, and their need to manufacture heroes, real saviours who will rescue them from the place of injustice and anonymity where they feel usually constrained—a desire that often colors their masturbatory fantasies. This, I think, is the basis for the incurable inclination of all women in all cultures towards romanticism: the need for someone else, the man, to take responsibility, to be in charge, to take over the custody of their sexuality because of the fear that such a great burden has on their egos. Romanticism is well linked with guilt, women's fear of exercising openly their powerful sexuality without having to hide behind the image of an apparent sexless scenario. Women, in general, feel more inclined than men towards religion and magic, because they feel more helpless, more guilty about the power of imprinting, plus they fear losing that special place mothers had designed for them of the "good sexless little girl," the "Little Red Riding Hood" hunted by the "Big Bad Wolf."[1] Women's consciousness appears to be more self-demanding, and often more self-accusing, than men's. For instance, they are more demanding in relation to cleanliness, appearance, order, perfection, dates, and so forth—some-

---

[1]From a comic strip: Someone approached Little Red Riding Hood and asked: "Miss Little Red Riding Hood?" She became angry and answered: "No, Mrs. Big Bad Wolf."

thing present from very early in life. We can see it in the difference of how notebooks are kept in primary school by boys and girls, and later on, in the capacity of women to remember all sorts of anniversaries. When such self-demand is exaggerated, and it is often, women feel guilty and insecure as a consequence of several causes:

a) because of the power of imprinting, the power of their bodies, as I have already mentioned;
b) the cloaca theory: the confusion between anal and vaginal functions;
c) the mother's identification with their daughters and tendency to exercise a greater sexual repression, mostly over masturbation; and
d) biological demands, such as monthly menstrual periods and risk of pregnancy.

In the United States, different from European countries, we have witnessed during recent years an increasing number of movies whose contents range from witchcraft or enchantments to life after death, ghosts, time disruption, special powers, such as ESP, telekinesis, telepathy, clairvoyance, and prophetic divination, which have been extremely appealing to the average public. I have the fantasy that such a special need to create this kind of "mythology" and the proneness to watch it is directly related to the difficult, frustrating, stressful, and everyday routine everyday life that most people have to face regularly in industrialized countries. Life has become so predictable, repetitious, organized, and boring that an immediate consequence might be the need for magic and esoteric powers, as a direct complication and a necessary outlet.[2]

When statistics reveal an increasing number of pregnancies among adolescents, because no necessary precautions were taken during intercourse, because they were "swept away," I think that these contemporary girls, who otherwise appear so responsible about their sex lives and careers, are just believing in pure magic, plain wish fulfill-

---

[2]Incidences of suicide among adolescents is higher in industrialized countries (usually Nordic) than in Third World ones (usually Equatorial). My belief is that long and harsh winters are a determining factor because such a threat does not exist in tropical countries. The winter demands a need for organization and careful and long-term planning because life itself is at stake. In tropical cultures, the climate is so benevolent that improvisation is not so dangerous and organization not so indispensable. Since most politicians in Latin American countries, for instance, suffer from "delusions of grandeur" whenever they reach power, they start at random, without any research or marketing whatsoever, multimillion dollar enterprises, which are often left unfinished by the time their term in power has come to an end. When the next politicians take over command, they also have the strong need to create something of their own and to "mark" their own territory, having to disregard, in their rush, whatever might have been commenced by their predecessor in order to start their own multimillion dollar project. Such a continuous doing and undoing leaves, like the myth of Sisyphus, no room for boredom, ceaselessly providing a very "juicy" hope about so many new things to create, leaving little room for suicide. This is different, of course, from Nordic cultures, where a demand for careful planning and continuous maintenance does not allow for improvisations, and adolescents usually feel useless and despaired once they discover the fatalistic fact that everything is already "done."

ment, just the desire that by the power invested in God everything will be as anticipated.

Such a need for witchcraft has always been present in all cultures since the beginning of time, perhaps less now than before, as a consequence of the continuous advance of science. A good example is the disappearance of well-known and universal specters such as the Headless Horseman, or the ghost defender of treasures, and so forth. Once Edison's great invention, the electrical light, illuminated the nights, most of these spooky visions vanished forever. But phantoms are not the only consequence of men's powerful inclination towards magic; there has also been a tendency to idealize and glorify earthly human beings, such as Buddha, Mohammad, Moses, Christ, or the Virgin Mary. This is why it would be considered irreverent to examine them by the light of common logic like that of any ordinary mortal. Let's think, for example, about a less controversial individual, such as the well-known Christopher Columbus who discovered America. He divorced his wife to marry a cartographer's daughter in order to have access to the world charts of his time. In addition, he gave away his only son, Diego, to the Ravida Convent for a period of time so he would not interfere with Columbus' desire to give himself completely to his enterprise. If we were to define normality according to any acceptable and average citizen's behavior, Columbus was not a model of ethics or a high moral paradigm. What kind of a person, in his or her right mind, would venture in a sailboat where nobody had ever risked sailing before, with a bunch of uncertain ex-convicts, through an ocean thought to be, by every educated person, completely flat and falling from the edge of the infinite to an incommensurable void? Even today, any normal human being would be more concerned about their business, politics, family, or how to win the lottery.

I can imagine Columbus going inside a tavern in Genoa, for instance, and opening the door while the other customers turn around to see who is coming and whisper: "Hey Giusseppe, look who's coming, that guy, Columbus. Don't let him see you, don't look at his eyes. If he sees us, he'll come over here with that old story that the earth is round and that you can go to India by the west, and all of that nonsense, and I am telling you, man, I can't take it any more. Listen Giusseppe, look man, oh no, he's coming this way, I shit on. . . ." Columbus arriving: "Good day gentlemen, how are you today? What are you drinking? Have I told you that my project is now completed and that the good king of Portugal feels very delighted about it? Did you know that if we navigate towards the west, we will arrive by the east?" *Total silence.*

It is true that history, on the other hand, has been decided by exceptional men. Julius Caesar, for instance, used to embitter himself as early as twenty-three-years-old because at this same age Alexander had conquered the whole world, "while he, Caesar, had done nothing." There is no doubt that such stubborn ambitiousness, abnormal to a certain extent, and such addiction to endless fame induced Alexander, Julius Caesar, Napoleon, Bolívar, Christ, and Hitler to find a place in history without discriminating, of course, whether it was for good, bad, selfish, or altruistic reasons.

I suspect that when Queen Isabella of Spain decided to sell her jewels in order to acquire the money for Columbus' journey, she did it, not because of her interest and knowledge about science, nor because her erudition about un-known oceans or undiscovered lands brought her to the absolute conviction that the earth was completely round, and that all scholars from her time, who thought other-wise, were a bunch of nitwits. Perhaps this poor queen was completely overwhelmed by the royal court's responsibil-ities, by the never ending war against the Moor infidels and other kingdoms, as well as her daughter Juana's ("La Loca") schizophrenia and her marital problems with her husband, Ferdinand. Perhaps because of those conditions, she could no longer tolerate Columbus' continuous, repe-titious, and persistent demands. Could anybody imagine a woman giving up her jewelry just like that, in order to procure money and invest it in an unknown individual, in an enterprise that even in these days would appear a bit daft? I suspect that with so many problems, Isabella sold her jewels and gave the money to Columbus, with the sole purpose of getting rid of him. After all, what kind of information did Isabella have about unknown worlds or remote oceans if most of the savants of her time assured her that the earth was completely flat, resting on top of four elephants, which were placed on the back of a gigantic turtle swimming in a sea of milk. The befuddled Isabella must have found it difficult to believe her ears, when, after several months of complete rest, perhaps fantasizing about Columbus' disappearance, along with the Santa Maria and the rest, in the depth of the milk ocean, she heard the announcement that Columbus was returning from the other side of the earth. America does not bear Columbus' name because he did not discover it—*he invented it.*

I think we believe in God because of two reasons, either out of *tradition* or by means of *transaction.* By tradition, I mean that we repeat whatever we were told, without questioning, just because our parents held certain beliefs, and we adopt these beliefs out of pure imitation. Or, in the face of infinitude, fear of death, and the great mystery of life, we resort to a transaction. If Christ, for instance, was a god, we shouldn't be surprised about his wisdom and great humanism. After all, everything should be easier for a god; but if, on the contrary, he was just another mortal like the rest of us, then he deserves superb recognition and deep admiration because of his immense sensibility and intelligence, so much so that humanity will be mentioning his name until the end of mankind. If Christ were a man, history could have been told in a different manner. One of the reasons that Christianity sold itself so well around the world[3] was because it offered, in the first place, the possibility of a better justice and a better "life" for men after death, and most important of all, it provided the possibility of a confession, a humanitarian and comprehensive form of forgiveness so that we could rid ourselves, around the clock, of any sin, regardless of how serious it might have been. And of course, one demonstration of the greatness of Jesus was that he died exactly for what he believed in, following his own doctrine and teaching; and that he did it without fear, and even without defending himself, in order to validate that everything he said about a better and more just life after death was true. Having to die, however, was not the real problem; the greatest difficulty was, I think, the "raising" of his soul to Heaven as genuine certification of a true eternity, a belief

---

[3]Judaism, on the other hand, has always been more discriminating than proselytizing.

that demanded the disappearance of his body. This event was so determining that it could have not been left entirely to chance; it required careful planning a long time before the crucifixion could have taken place. I think that the Bible gives us some clues:

a) Christ "called" on Simon, a fisherman born in Bethsaida, and changed his name to the Greek "Cephas" or Peter, signifying "rock." I think that rock has two qualities: it is not only *hard* but it is also *silent*;

b) At a given moment, Christ said that Peter was the rock on which he would build his church, and that he would give him the keys to the Kingdom of Heaven (Matthew 16:17–19). We could interpret this by saying that he meant that he would build his church on the unconditional trust he felt for Peter's capacity to remain "silent";

c) What was the purpose of Christ's asking Peter to deny him three times before crucifixion? Was it a test to see if Peter was capable of lying, and to do it out of pure obedience?; and

d) Christ said too, that whatever was said by Peter on Earth would be also said by him in Heaven, meaning perhaps that Peter would always be telling the truth even if he lied!

Let's imagine that Christ asked Peter, his friend and follower, to take over the macabre concern of hiding his remains. Maybe, since Peter was a fisherman, he could throw it into the sea and then specifically attest, as he did, that his master had risen to the sky. After all, Peter, together with brothers James and John, formed part of the "inner ring" that alone witnessed Jesus' raising of Jairus's daughter from the dead, and was also the first to see the rising Christ (Mark 5:22, 1 Cor. 15:5). I think that if it was difficult for Jesus to die for what he believed in, it must have been twice as difficult for Peter to be fated for the rest of his life to keep a secret he could never reveal to anyone. We can imagine Peter's long nights of insomnia, terrified of giving away his secret while sleeping, or perhaps the fear of temptation, for narcissistic reasons, to show off with friends the fact that he was chosen by his master for such a transcendental task. Or the dread of drinking too much and under the effect of inebriation betraying the mission imposed upon him, or maybe sharing it with his wife as an existential need of freeing himself from the burden of a terrible loneliness, of being the only one in the whole world in possession of such a commitment. I think that the real martyrdom of Peter was the transcendental and absolute loneliness of his *silence*. After all, what good is a secret that cannot be shared? In summary, there are several parameters we should consider that plot against women's identity and lower their self-esteem:

a) The identification of mothers with their daughters and their need to exercise control over their sexuality, masturbation in particular;
b) The confusion over the vaginal role, between excretory and orgastic functions;
c) The guilt about women's power of imprinting; and
d) Their hidden genitalia, creating the unconscious feeling of absence.

All of these disorientations that I have discussed in detail in previous chapters cheat women out of their own rights and interfere with the possibility of structuring an inner feeling of security, of a high self-esteem. Such insecurity induces the need to search for answers outside of themselves, to idealize and envy men's prerogatives, to attack and denigrate women's attributes; it increases the need to depend on men, to give themselves blindly, to be "swept away," to believe in saviors and to resort to magic. I do not believe that magic is synonymous with femininity, but I do believe that women resort to these kind of answers more often than men do.[4]

---

[4]*See* Nancy Friday, 1991, *Women on Top*. New York: Pocket Star Books.

# 12    ALCHEMY

Merit is not in the golden crown, but to have peace in our
thoughts.

—Lope de Vega

The control of religious mysticism during the Medieval
Dark Ages not only restrained any possibility of scientific
development, but also provoked and maintained the predominance of an esoteric milieu, pervaded with witchcraft
and sorcery, where both magic and science were exercised
and confused undiscriminatingly. In search of the *philosopher's stone*, men hidden in dark and humid castle
cellars recited magic and ancient formulas while scorching
and churning the "matter," a mixture of metals and filth.
They were capable of producing, without distinction,
chemical amalgamations and compounds compatible with
modern chemistry, as well as marvelous and miraculous

elixirs competent enough to subdue the most quarrelsome love or the most dangerous enemy.

Although alchemy was a pseudo-science concerned with changing base metals such as lead or copper into silver or gold, it was also linked with the roots of chemistry itself. In a document from the Middle Ages, Eximenes, a mid-century Spanish philosopher, alerted ingenuous people about the alchemist's art and the possibility of being deceived: *"You ought to escape from the alchemists, who are usually mad, deceivers, quick to spend what is not theirs, who never deliver what they promised and who never bring themselves to give up or to lose, and who always have incarnated that pestilence and can never move away from it."*[1]

Alchemy was universal, and Arabs as well as Chinese, Greeks, and Romans practiced it equally around the same time, revealing the existence of a collective unconscious concern, in a Jungian sense. I believe that alchemy represented the need for men to reverse the "narcissistic injury" when they were exposed to babies, which I have already referred to in the previous chapter: the primary suspiciousness and mistrust generated by a terrible deceit, that what the adults wanted so much for the baby to provide, inducing the feeling that it was as valuable as gold, was just pure pestilence. *Alchemy perhaps represented an inverse operation, the desire to convert whatever was suffered*

---

[1]*"E per tal deuen molt esquiuar alquimistas qui comunament son orats e enganadors e guastadors del seu e null temps no venen a fi daço que volen e veense fondre e perdre e son axi encarnats in aquella pestilencia que ya james no sen volen lunyar."* Regiment de Princeps, Chap. 379.

*during the "narcissistic injury" from childhood into some-*
*thing of value; the possibility of finally changing feces into*
*gold, in order to revert the terrible humiliation they were*
*exposed to as children.* Although alchemy could not satisfy
such a desire, it did manage to deliver, through the never
ending search for the philosopher's stone, the secret combinations of different elements, the transmutation of "va-
lences" from one compound to another, which, at the end,
established the basis for modern chemistry. Perhaps alchemists were not capable of solving the mysterious, hermetic
secret of mutating feces into gold, but they were capable of
accomplishing the sublimation of that infantile desire by
producing the foundation for contemporary science: they
did not find the metallic gold, but the symbolic "gold" of
science and creativity.

In this sense, true alchemists do exist as men who
have been able to extract the *maximum* from *nothing-*
*ness*, which is, I think, the real expression of a genius's
creation. Let's take, for instance, the story of Sir Alexander
Fleming who, in 1928, by accident and shrewd observation, discovered the antibiotic power of penicillin.

Not long ago, diagnosis and treatment of infectious
diseases were made with the use of cultures in special
plates containing material such as agar,[2] which required
careful handling by lab technicians. For instance, taking a
smear from the throat required a gas burner nearby, in
order to kill bacteria in the air and thus avoid the danger of
contamination. When this was not properly executed,
contaminated cultures usually showed a transparent halo

---

[2]A gelatinous extractive of red alga, used in laboratories to
plant bacteria in order to examine them.

around the colonies. When examined under the microscope, they found that the bacteria were dead, the test useless, and thus the smear had to be repeated, perhaps after scolding the "negligent" technician and throwing the culture away. Nobody, however, before Fleming, had the curiosity to ask a simple question: What sort of organism present in the air was responsible for such total destruction of bacteria and, could it also work on a living person? A professor of mine at McGill University (Montreal, Canada) told me once that he remembered Hanz Selye recriminating himself for being so careless and not paying enough attention to the same phenomenon Fleming observed, which he also had seen so many times before.[3]

When Sir Fleming investigated the bacteria's cause of death in the agar cultures, he found that they were invaded by the common green mold widespread in the air, which usually strikes any food left unsheltered. Sir Fleming baptized the mold with the sophisticated name of *Penicillium notatum,* and discovered that it produced a substance that not only dissolved the infectious bacteria, but was also non-toxic to humans.

What everyone considered, and still do, a vulgar green mold, an unpleasant nuisance that spoils food and changes it into pure garbage stuff, was suddenly commuted by the shrewd observation of Sir Fleming, one of the greatest

---

[3]It seems ironic that Hanz Selye, a very creative investigator who, back in the fifties, introduced in medicine the now popular concept of *stress*, and who also founded the International Institute of Stress at the Université de Montreal, died about nine years ago from heart failure three months after the Revenue Office of Canada informed him that he owed approximately $150,000.00 in back taxes from previous donations.

alchemists of our modern time. He managed to invert the "narcissistic injury," and finally achieved what so many had attempted but failed to do: *to transform spoils and death into pure life.* The unwelcome green mold not only provided Sir Fleming with a title of nobility, but also indisputably contributed to his becoming the hero of this century, because antibiotics have been the greatest discovery in modern time, completely changing the outcome of medicine.

Sigmund Freud is another contemporary alchemist who established that the doors to the unconscious, the most powerful and determining side of the human mind, are clearly elicited by everyday common dreams or spontaneous thoughts, usually intimate, other times shameful, which normally are forgotten shortly after they take place, or metaphorically, thrown into the waste basket of oblivion.

Alchemy, as one can see, is not just the product of magic thinking that dominated the ignorant mind of medieval men, who were convinced, by the derangement of their imagination, that secret formulas or specific combinations of certain substances could provide the most astounding wealth, once they changed the pestilence into gold. Alchemy arose as a marvelous manifestation of the dark and powerful energy of the unconscious, as a search for the hero, who, armed with the philosopher's stone, would domesticate the deep forces of unconscious creativity in order to change *nothingness into everything.*

Alchemy appears as an exalted or sublimated need to search for a way out from the determining shame elicited by feces, from humiliation and distrust, to find the mysterious and symbolical secret of transmutation, to change feces into gold. It seems quite paradoxical that not only human intimacy, as we expressed before, is attached and determined by anal influences, but that creativity too, the capacity of obtaining "everything out of nothing," is also directly conditioned by the sublimation of feces.

The reason I have included the present chapter in this essay about women is because I believe that a continuous search for creativity within the spirit of femininity will finally bring women to find their proper identity, to find what Merlin Stone and other co-writers have designated as the *universal feminine principle*, the real transcendence and true mutation, not just senseless magic and searching for the answer outside of oneself. The alchemy of this universal principle will generate a deep and serious shift towards inner growth, self-sufficiency, independence, and coexistence, not through rivalry and competition, but through compatibility with her natural partners: men. I will insist on this aspect of transcendence in the chapter dedicated to the "Vindicated Eve," but before I do that, let's review an important subject: the difference between a historical and a biological concept of God.

# 13   TOTEM AND TABOO: FROM GOD-MAN TO GOD-WOMAN

And the rib, which the Lord God had taken from man, made he a woman and brought her unto the man. And Adam said, 'This is now bone of my bone, and flesh of my flesh; she shall be called Woman, because she was taken out of Man.'

—Genesis 2:22–23

In 1913, Freud published his well-known contribution to the fields of anthropology and sociology under the title of *Totem and Taboo*, in which he attempted to investigate the phylogenetic basis of the Oedipus Complex, as well as the sociological understanding of religion, based on observation of both animal behavior and primitive people. Originally, he said, men organized themselves in a manner similar to mammals that live in groups, such as wild horses, buffaloes, monkeys, or sea lions, among others, as they do today. They are patriarchal societies with a domineering male who not only protects the herd from any outside menace, but also acts as the absolute master of all females, fiercely guarding his dominion from any younger male (usually his own offspring), who easily yields to his authority. But at any given moment, however, the most primitive and universal conspiracy takes place—perhaps the expression of the most primeval revolution—when all the males get together and one of them, maybe the strongest, most courageous, challenges the domineering father to a mortal duel. After his death or defeat, the new victor becomes the ruling male. In primitive societies, the death of the father produced terrible feelings of guilt and "paranoid anxiety." After all, the father not only had given life to his progeny, but had provided for them and protected them as well. The guilt produced the fantasy that the father, after his death and from the "place where he dwells," would take a dreadful revenge, inducing the need to pacify his soul by means of different rituals, which according to Freud, became the basis for the origin of all religions. They would, for instance, incinerate his body to make certain that he was not going to return, and then ingest the ashes in a ceremony to make the dead father part of themselves. This could be associated with the principle implicit in the communion of the Christian faith as well as other religions. *Not being completely convinced of his death, they then glorified and venerated his memory, giving place in this manner to the origin of God.* However, the magnitude of the guilt was such that their attempts at finding a protective mechanism always failed, forcing them to search for other alternatives, such as the need of repeating forever all the details of the conspiracy as a form of expiation. The dead father was then represented by a totem or by a certain animal, forbidden to be touched, hurt, or hunted except during a definite period of the year, when all the members of the tribe organized themselves in order to kill the animal, as a symbolical repetition of the original deed in which they did really murder their father. After the hunt, the ceremony was then consummated with a "totemic meal" or communion, where they all ate the animal. The Israelis, for example, use the lamb, while the Christians use the fish, representing Christ, as the only food allowed during the yearly ceremonial of Easter, when his death is commemorated.[1]

This hypothesis, formulated by Freud, obviously links *men* to the image of God as the glorified representation of the murdered father. This obviously contradicts the proposal introduced in this essay, which states that if God were to have a sex, it would be a female. I think, however, that such discrepancy is only in appearance, and that the difference between the two theories depends more on a historical or evolutionary perspective than on the form in which they were formulated. Freud's *Totem and Taboo* presents a social and historical point of view, which deciphers with great logic the origin of religions. Imprinting, on the other hand, is an instinctive and biological phenomenon that tries to explain not only man's envy of women and his need to subdue them until now, but also women's attempt to achieve a more prominent position during times

---

[1]Pictorial representations of fish can still be seen in some of the Roman catacombs as an early Christian identification, maybe because Christ was conceived as a "fisherman of souls," or perhaps portraying Peter's trade, one of the most relevant disciples at the beginning of Christianity. The image of the Pope when seen from one side, wearing the mitre (like a fish's open mouth) and a silver cloak (like the scales), resembles the shape of a fish.

to come. If the beginning of humanity was dominated by magic and religion, the future will be ruled by the power of scientific and logical reasoning. I say, then, that if the God of all religions originated from a primitive organization of men, similar to those observed at present in the social organization of animals, it *must be a male God;* while the God of the future, based on the real and logical power of biology, built on the successive growth of women, on their greater awareness and relevance, *must be a female God.*

Ortega-y-Gasset, the Spanish philosopher, once said that the difference between a person and a tiger was that the latter could never "de-tigerize" itself. It is fatalistically condemned to be a *tiger* forever, contrary to men, who are capable of questioning and transcending everything, as one can see in the merciless "ontological peeling" of men and humanity that existentialism has taught us. It has been said that science has given three fundamental blows to men's pride and to religion: in the first place, it has proven that the sun, and not the earth, occupies the center of our universe; second, that according to evolutionism, humans share common roots with the monkeys; and finally, that most of the human mind is unconsciously hidden. Not long ago I wrote:

> *It would be unnatural, and even naive, to imagine that any given institution could remain unchanged in the face of entropy of continuous historical changes and new revealing knowledge. However, if at a given time, someone were to have inquired about the future to a third century B.C. Roman centurion, he most certainly would have assured him that the Roman Empire was going to be there forever. It was*

*not by chance that he had witnessed, for more than three hundred years, the succession of one emperor after the other.*

*The world was not the same after Aristotelian "crystal spheres" and heavenly bodies stumbled down—pushing God to other boundaries—under Copernicus' intuition and Galileo's telescope. Not even the Inquisition's terrorizing secular arm could prevent those innovations. Neither could Genesis's Adam and Eve determinism uphold any longer the comfort religion had offered men when confronted with the hard and violent, but unquestionable logical reasoning of Darwin's evolutionism: humans and monkeys were closely related. The Earth was no longer the center of the Universe, and MAN was not God's spoiled and favored creation. The revelation of the unconscious by Freud at the end of the last century introduced the third great shame: Men were similar to the iceberg—one-tenth rational, and nine-tenths submerged parts of abject and pure unknown animality. The Earth: a small rock lost in the immensity of an infinite space. Man: the monkey's first cousin, psychologically and sociologically behaving like one of them most of the time. But even so, we should not feel too pessimistic. On the contrary, these revelations have been quite useful, because they have helped us discover the exact and secure location where truth continuously places us, to such a point that new advances are really unbelievable. Thanks to electronics the Earth is just a small village (Marshall McLuhan's words); we no longer fear, like in ancient times, the threat of plague, and we live in such comfort that a medieval man could have never imagined. . .*[2]

---

[2]Read at the Venezuelan Psychoanalytical Association, July, 1993.

"Totem and Taboo" refers mostly to the early origins of mankind, establishing an analogy between the organization of primitive people and the society of certain mammals, to which we, human beings, are biologically related. It also refers to religion's *phallocratic* preponderance, because the genesis of all churches is interrelated with aboriginal man's magical way of thinking, to his need of dominating and controlling his environment with the use of brutal force in order to survive, to establish a patriarchy, and to submissively surrender all women as an object of commerce and exclusive providers of pleasure. This is why *patrimony* is related to property or heritage, while *matrimony* is identified with carnal union.

Up to the moment of Freud's death, *Totem and Taboo* constituted for him the ontogenetic and phylogenetic basis for a biological corroboration of the Oedipus Complex. However, Melanie Klein, the psychoanalyst who probably introduced the most significant contributions to psychoanalysis since Freud, presented a different conception of such a complex. According to her, it was already present from very early on, even before the child could differentiate the sexes. For Klein, the Oedipus Complex is more a direct consequence of the "original triad": mother, father, and child, where the child is always exposed to *exclusion,* something that usually generates a great amount of anxiety. In other words, the center of the Oedipus Complex—its most unconscious component—is not so much the rivalry between the child and the parent of the same sex, as well as the search for the other of the opposite sex. Instead, it is the need to avoid the terrible pain of exclusion: "Two are company, but three are a crowd," says the popular expression.

The hypothesis, which states that imprinting will determine the future relevance of women, demonstrates the predominance of biology and scientific logic over any other form of human argumentation. It will decide the place rational thinking will occupy in the future, once the magic obscurantism of religion and primitive reasoning is replaced by the prospect of a scientific rationale. *If a "man-God" was, up to now, the product of a religious tradition, a "woman-God" will be the product of biology's unavoidable determinism in the future.*

# 14 FEMININITY

Tiresias, who was both man and woman, was asked to mediate in a dispute between Jove and Juno over who, men or women, got more pleasure out of sex. He answered: 'if you could divide pleasure into tenths, nine would be for the woman, and only one for the man.'

—Ovid

Man has never been able to understand or accept completely two phases of humanity: the mystery of its beginning, and the dread of its end. The first is related with the origin of mankind, its capacity to beget, to bear life, or in other words to perform *sex*. The second one is connected with the end of men, their definite and final disappearance from life, with *death*. Both dimensions are the expression of men's basic instinctive duality: *Eros* (love, creativity, and life) and *Thanatos* (aggression, destruction, and death).

The impossibility of ever getting used to sex, inciting us to continuously witness it as if we had never seen it before, and observe the repetitious execution of a coitus, as if it were for the first time, guarantees not only procreation, but also, as a complication, the existence of *pornography.* The fear of death, on the other hand, as we never get accustomed to its reality, brings about the need for *religion*, always repetitive and dogmatic, *which continuously applies ancient books and old cultures to a modern era, as if time had not elapsed.* The ugly consequence of this fear is perpetual religious warfare for the supremacy of each group's particular God. This is why pornography and religion might have a common enemy: boredom and the monotonous repetition of always being absolutely the same.

It is quite difficult for people to allow changes to take place because there exists an inborn tendency to persistently adhere to old norms and practices, and a horror of the unknown, of what is to come. Something that appears to be an absolute truth today could be a lie tomorrow, and a complete nuisance in the hereafter. Many definitions of femininity will also break down as time passes, once we prove that such characteristics are just cultural and not completely genetic, and will change as science and new psychological discoveries are accomplished. At the present time, women are less masochistic than in the past, more sure of their own rights, and more competitive—completely different, for instance, from those descriptions portrayed by sacred and ancient books still venerated, regardless of the time when they were written: "All women are wicked," said Buddha. "If they have the opportunity, they will sin." And Saint Ambrose, bishop of Milan in the year A.D. 374 once said: "Because women induced men to sin, it is fair that they receive men like the slave receives the king." Even more, it appears that the continuous degradation of women is a common argument in all religious books. "To the woman," said God: "And I will multiply your work and miseries with pregnancies, and in pain shall ye bring forth children, and you will be under the dominion of your husband, and he will dominate you . . .", says the Bible in Genesis (Gen. 3:16), and again in Deuteronomy (24:1): "When a man hath taken a wife, and married her, and it come to pass that she find no favour in his eyes, because he hath found some uncleanness in her, then let him write her a bill of divorcemente, and give it in her hand, and send her out of his house." Saint Paul said: "That women keep silence when in church. . . . If they need to be instructed on any matter, ask their husband when at home. Because it is indecent for a woman to talk in church . . . and it was not Adam the one seduced, but Eve, who, seduced committed transgression" (1 Corinthians 14:34–35). The Koran, on the other hand expressed: "Give to men double of what you give to women. . . . Men are superior to women, because God has given them pre-eminence over women. Husbands who suffer disobedience from their wives should punish them, leave them alone in their beds and even hit them. . . . If to any of them the birth of a daughter is announced, his face gets gloomy and he gets choked with the pain. . . . He hides from his family because of the terrible news" (Sura IV, Vers. 11, 38; Sura XVI, Vers. 60, 61). Meanwhile Manu, the sacred book of India, states: "It is in the nature of women to attempt to corrupt all men here on earth, and this is why no wise men ever give themselves to any women's seduction. (Laws of

Manu: Book II, Rule No. 213). . . . Even if the husband's demeanor is questionable, even if there are other lovers and he lacks good qualities, virtuous women should continuously venerate them before God (Book V, Rule No. 154). . . . A barren woman should be replaced after the eighth year; the one who lost all the children, on the tenth; the one who only conceived girls, on the eleventh; and the one who speaks with acrimony, immediately" (Book IX, Rule No. 81). "I thank thee, O Lord, that thou hast not created me a woman," relates the Daily Orthodox Jewish book of prayer, while Pythagoras (5th Century B.C.) said: "There is good principle which created order, light and man, and an evil principle which created chaos, darkness, and women." Seneca (c. 4 B.C.–A.D. 65), the Spanish philosopher, expressed: "When a woman thinks, she thinks evil." "The five worst infirmities that afflict the female are indocility, discontent, slander, jealousy and silliness. . . . Such is the stupidity of woman's character, that it is incumbent upon her, in every particular, to distrust herself and to obey her husband," states the Confucian book of marriage.

The invention of the nursing bottle to feed babies has made it possible for women's presence to no longer be essential as the "wet nurse," and for men to be able to participate in nursing. By the same token, the creation of new and safer methods of contraception have provided more freedom to all women. One can argue, for instance, that *menstruation* and *pregnancy* are both authentic and specific definitions of womanhood, however, it is quite possible that in the future new discoveries in the field of physiology or computerized biology could make it possible for these apparent distinctive characteristics to become optional.

Never could Alexander the Great imagine the invention of rocket bombs, or Leonardo da Vinci the creation of supersonic jets, or Gutenberg the advent of computers. What other future inventions might we find difficult to believe now? Twice, before the complete disarticulation of the USSR, the Russians publicly accused the Americans of being responsible for the existence of HIV, as a result of genetic engineering experiments with the purpose of finding new biological methods for the control of tissue rejection after organ transplant operations. The subjects for the experiment were perhaps homosexuals and Haitian volunteers, who were considered free of danger after some three years of observation, without knowing at that time that HIV needed a longer period in order to produce AIDS.

It is quite possible to imagine that some time from now, women will have the option of not becoming pregnant, choosing instead the alternative of "computerized uterus banks," where babies are conceived and raised until they are ready for delivery, giving them also the opportunity to select sex, color, IQ, and so on in advance. If all of these specific characteristics of womanhood were to become optional, what then will remain basic and unique as an unmistakable definition of femininity?

Tiresias, the great soothsayer of Greek mythology, was paradoxically blind as the consequence of Gaia's rage (Gaia the earth, as the paradigm of womanhood), because Tiresias, being a hermaphrodite, was able to reveal women's greatest secret. When questioned about who enjoyed orgasm more, women or men, Tiresias answered: "If you could divide pleasure into tenths, nine would be for the woman, and only one for the man" (Morgan 1970, p. 197).

*Memory* represents the essential characteristic that defines identity and individuality for each human being. In the future, for instance, we might be able to transplant all sorts of organs, including the brain, without necessarily changing the specific identity of a person; however, the only thing that can never be changed is the specific place that harbors the memory, because essentially we are nothing more than just water and history. *Orgasm*, similar to memory, is what basically differentiates masculinity from femininity, because any other function can be either interchanged or left aside, but not the act of penetration or being penetrated. At the end, and as a result of what I have said so far, we could conclude that femininity could be essentially defined under three basic conditions:

   a) the power of imprinting and how it is administrated
      by women;
   b) the internal distribution of her sexual organs; and
   c) the characteristics of orgasm.

But there is one last detail we should consider: *the hymen*, that frail and mysterious membrane that partially obstructs the vagina from birth, whose purpose is still a riddle to the biologist as well as to the anthropologist, and which seems to be as useful as a freezer to an Eskimo. Its real nature might never be completely understood: whether it is for protection against parasites creeping inside the vagina or against the penis for the same reason, or both. The only thing that the hymen has been useful for is the humiliation of women—more in the past than at the present time—as a way for a man to know if his wife has had previous sexual experience, to find out about the consummation of marriage, or for parents who, fearful of their daughter's "sinful" sexuality, felt the right to probe her intimacy on the gynecologist's table.

I have stated in previous chapters that the natural tendency of mothers to identify with their daughters usually induces a more critical attitude about them, more than they might have about their boys. The mothers seem to project onto the daughters their own fears and limitations, not knowing exactly towards whom such interest is directed, towards the girls or themselves, out of love or pure selfishness. The main target of this controlling attitude is sex, mostly masturbation, inducing the fear in the little girl that such procedure is bad, dirty, sinful, and so forth. This belief later on creates in the unconscious of many women the symbolical structure of the "prostitute-nun": the feeling of being trapped between powerful instinctive needs on one hand, and strong sentiments of guilt on the other. Nancy Friday recently stressed the importance of masturbation in women because its regular practice increments a sense of self-hood, of separation from the others, and serves not only as a tool to distinguish between pure sex and love—as she feels men are capable of doing—but also as an exercise to enrich sexual fantasies and to improve performance during coitus. *"Last and most obvious,"* she says *"masturbation is one of life's greatest sources of sexual pleasure, thrilling in itself, a release from tension, a sweet sedative before sleep, a beauty treatment that leaves us glowing, our countenance more tranquil, our smile more mysterious"* (1991, p. 35). As I stated before, women often confuse masturbation with intimacy, and experience it as something to be hidden. Modern women might talk freely with their friends and partners about any sexual subject. However, their masturbatory habits, including their fantasies, are always under strict inner censorship and, as a consequence, very seldom shared. I believe that the main problem consists in the restriction exercised by parents against masturbation, the anger that this prohibition elicited, together with the feeling that every time they perform it, they are not just enjoying themselves, they are also unconsciously "attacking" their parents by contravening their code of ethics. This is why Freud found certain symbolical analogy between masturbation and drug addiction.

# 15   Confused Eve

Women's advances and retreats are generally described in military terms: battles won, battles lost, points and territory gained and surrendered.

—Susan Faludi

I have already stated in previous chapters that we might presently be living the beginning of the "Confused Eve's" era. Even in Latin American countries, women no longer behave as they did in the past, and are fighting for their rights, trying to escape from the forced ignominy of previous centuries, and trying courageously to purify and modify their image as illegal, demonic, and dangerous people. But it has not been an easy search, because in that pursuit of a *universal feminine principle*, women have been guided by forces of chance, some biological, others cultural, which have fatalistically oriented them to the easiest way, towards the external appearance of men, to the fascination of the Other, of external masculinity, instead of the difficult quest for their own internal femininity. "Confused Eve" has fallen into the trap placed by biology, in the apparent idealized phallic domination, ignoring the more difficult but truthful investigation of her own hidden identity: fascinated by the phallus and appalled by their natural vaginal "wound," which they experience more as an absence than as a presence.

In recent years, women have been able to attain positions that were not only dominated by men in the past, but were forbidden to them; now women can vote and obtain important positions in business as well as politics. But most of these benefits, which women have fought hard for and achieved, have not helped them to get closer to their own femininity. On the contrary, they often seem to be induced by a competition with men, experiencing femininity as a void and masculinity as something to be imitated. Women now, for instance, feel suspicious about any attempt from men to treat them differently, and usually respond with indignation if the car door is opened or dinner is paid for by the male companion, to the point that even a compliment is experienced as sexual harassment or as a form of belittlement. This, I believe, is why women's liberation movements have failed in the past, creating a situation feminist Susan Faludi has referred to as backlash:

> *A backlash against women's rights is nothing new in American history. Indeed, it's a recurring phenomenon: it returns every time women begin to make some headway toward equality, a seemingly inevitable early frost to the culture's brief flowering of feminism. . . . The American woman is trapped on this asymptotic spiral, turning endlessly through the*

> *generations, drawing ever nearer to her destination*
> *without ever arriving. Each revolution promises to be*
> *'the revolution' that will free her from the orbit, that*
> *will grant her, finally, a full measure of human*
> *justice and dignity."* [1991, pp. 46–47]

And writer Ann Douglas also said: "The progress of women's rights in our culture, unlike other types of progress has always been strangely reversible" (1977, p. 199).

Such statements derive from the fact that so far, women have attempted to achieve their freedom from the outside, as if the responsibility for these accomplishments were the other's, as if the solution should come from the exterior, from men and not from the inner transformation of womanhood. John Taylor has recently described this condition as the "don't blame me" culture of victimization: "It's a strange phenomenon, this growing compulsion of Americans of all creeds, colors, and incomes, of the young and the old, the infirm and robust, the guilty as well as the innocent, to ascribe to themselves the status of victims to try to find someone or something else to blame for whatever is wrong or incomplete or just plain unpleasant about our life" (1991, p. 26).

*If masculinity is exalted and femininity devaluated, we could deduce that women will be successively masculinized.* Statistics show that many diseases, once more common among men, are now frequent among women, such as heart ailments and lung cancer. Endometriosis, on the other hand, is much more widespread than before, a disorder consisting of the presence of functioning endometrial tissue in places where it should not exist, or in other words, the tendency to menstruate inside of the body instead of allowing the normal menstrual blood to flow to the exterior, as all women do—a mechanism that psychologically indicates a feminine protest.

It is possible to think that if women become more masculinized, they might, consequently, feminize their male offspring. We can witness this nowadays in the behavior of many male youths, who have a tendency to let their hair grow and wear earrings, and in the increment of sexual ambiguity, among other things. However, it could also induce a paradoxical response, the increment of a compensatory male aggressiveness or macho type of behavior.

A few years ago, we witnessed a sequence of incidents during the European soccer tournament in which the protagonists were British youths, who on several occasions displayed such awful aggression that the game ended, not only with police intervention, but with several Italians dead. My notion at that moment was that perhaps the exaggerated British reaction against other nationalities was a compensatory macho response because their main leaders at that time were women: Mrs. Thatcher and Queen Elizabeth. Freud stated long ago that man's aggression might be linked to the fear of castration, a fear already incremented by the vision of woman's absence of a penis. The British youths, not having a powerful headman to emulate, unconsciously decided to place the "castration" on people from other latitudes, as they seemed to be saying with their sadistic intervention: "You are the castrated ones, not us."

This same dynamic appears to be present in warfare, always invented and carried out by men, never by women, with the exception of a few cases in which they were imitating men, or because specific historical circumstances forced them to do so. Even more, most pacifist movements are usually carried out by women. At this particular moment, due to the geniality of Gorbachev, we are living during a juncture of peace, and if it lasts long enough, the problem we will have to face in the future will be determined by lack of food due to the world's imminent overpopulation.

Christian philosophy continuously exalted pacifism to the extreme: "Do not judge if you do not wish to be judged," "Love your enemies and bless the one who curses you" were concepts preached by Jesus; and in his kindness there was no room for circumcision, perhaps the closest act to a true emasculation.

The search for a formula to finally abolish circumcision might have been present in the mind of Christ, and that is why John the Baptist became one of the greatest revelations for Christ's marvelous intuition, because John's discovery was a marvelous solution to deal with the problem of the "original sin" in the Old Testament. After John the Baptist, such a sin could be *washed* instead of *incised*. After all, from an unconscious point of view, to wash or to cut whatever we consider sinful has exactly the same connotation. I think that Christ's greatest and most important legacy for future generations that followed after him was the *foreskin*.

At the present time, there is a movement that has risen within medical circles, contrary to Jesus' superior contribution, preaching the need for circumcision for hygienic reasons. We could think, however, that such a practice must have been justified in the past for people living in the high temperatures of the desert, as they had scarce sources of fresh water for washing. But there is always the question that if this threat was really so determining, how could John the Baptist's and Christ's humanitarian dispositions have exceeded the danger of a body ailment? The deep and extreme feeling of frustration little boys must experience during the moment of circumcision (or to witness it when performed on younger brothers) must generate a grave sense of impotence and humiliation—leaving out pain—as well as a real threat, *because circumcision is so close to the real act of castration.* It is an action, on the other hand, only possible because of the natural helplessness of the child, which allows him to be subdued by the greater strength of the adults in order "to be castrated." I gather there must be a relationship between circumcision as a lessened ritual, and the sacrifice of children to Moloch, an early divinity Hebrews worshipped before Moses, by crushing children's heads against a rock. *I think that circumcision represents the most primitive and bloody religious ritual practiced in modern times.*

I also suspect that the difficulty of a double identity many Jews still experience is originated by the practice of such a ritual, which I hesitate to call symbolical due to its closeness to the real act of castration. During this ritual, circumcised fathers sustain the circumcision of their male offspring while the mother's passive participation is part of the conspiracy. The feeling of terror and immense desolation experienced by the child during this ceremony must induce a deep distrust, because both parents suddenly become executioners. This situation perhaps is similar to the shocking dread Isaac must have endured when confronted with Abraham's knife, with Sara never formulating any protest. Such a feeling of loneliness, desolation, and abandonment leads to a profound feeling of betrayal in the victim, of not belonging. The trust disappears because the parents, the greatest source of natural reliance we all experienced as children, have reverted, and even the mother, symbolically representing the greatest sense of belonging, has become alienated. After all, the mother, symbolically *Gaia* the earth, home, or motherland, is indispensable in order to structure a medullary sense of identity, of pertaining or belonging. When the mother herself is suspected of treason, it might unconsciously induce the need to search for some kind of belonging as a compensation, for an idealized or *promised land*, propitious of trust and hope. Something similar must take place with the father, who is also idealized and experienced as the Messiah, one who is always awaited—a sentiment that subsides once it is believed he might "have arrived." Then, with great surprise, he is no longer considered the Messiah. The fantasy of the ever "errant Jew" might have evolved as a consequence of this conflict.

In the act of circumcision, we could also perceive the presence of unconscious "philicide" tendencies, or the mother's unconscious wish to kill her own child, a concept emphasized by the Argentinean psychoanalyst, Arnoldo Ravskosky, which I have also referred to in the past as the "Isaac Complex." I suspect that the "talion law" (*lex talionis*)— "an eye for an eye and a tooth for a tooth"—which rules the unconscious, is present in that eternal and bloody struggle between Arabs and Jews, both circumcised. It seems, in a certain way, that such a fight might have some connection to the loss of the *foreskin*, as if each party was accusing the other of being responsible for the "castration." *It is like a perpetual war because of the incapacity to mourn the loss of the foreskin.*

When Freud described the concept of "penis envy" in women and the "castration complex" in men, he was responding to his own observation about the psychological profile of patients he treated at the turn of this century. Women's thinking corresponded more with the characteristics of the "Confused Eve," different from the "Delinquent Eve's" previous era, where the most important unconscious factor was men's envy over maternity and their defensive need to identify women with the demon itself.

The change from one "Eve" to the other was not only the consequence of women's continuous struggle, but also of the emergence of scientific reflection. When men became aware, due to new discoveries in microscopic observations, that they were also an indispensable part of the act of procreation, that envy toward women's maternity lessened and they accepted more their masculine role, feeling reassured about their indubitable paternity: now men are fathers and not just simple spectators or witnesses. As their envy decreased, not only did their need to subdue women and to compete with them diminish,[1] but also this change in attitude helped Eve's conversion from "Delinquent" to "Confused," as her demonic image and her ignominy from other times dissipated. Women exchanged submission, humiliation, and shame for phallic idealization, as envy had switched proprietor from men to women. The future change from "Confused" to "Vindicated Eve"

---

[1]Lets think, for instance, about men's clothing, make-up, and affectation around the French Court during the sixteenth and seventeenth centuries.

will depend not so much on the relationship between men and women, *but on women themselves, in their capacity to search inside without fear, to find the genuine roots of their own identity, their hidden sexuality, the power of imprinting and the legal rightness for their own intellect.*

# 16 ADAM

I see the phenomenon of what I would call the "soft male" all over the country today. Sometimes when I look out at my audiences, perhaps half the young males are what I'd call soft.

—Robert Bly

Man's superiority will be shown, not in the fact that he has enslaved his wife, but that he has set her free.

—Eugene V. Debs

It is highly significant that so many books have been written about femininity and rarely anything has been said about masculinity, as if the first one required so many explanations and the latter so few. Masculinity is so obvious and visible, without retaining any obscure enigma, while femininity is so obscure, hidden and mysterious, that such a discrepancy in scientific as well as neophyte information is absolutely understandable; either male concreteness does not inspire the same curiosity, or female masochism induces many writers, male as well as female, to rescue women from their historical opprobrium.

As I stated previously, men's tangible sexuality certainly influences their way of thinking, because they do not need any kind of abstraction to figure out their own identity. Also they do not have to face the threat of menstruation, virginity, or pregnancy; and their sexuality is more openly exercised because it is supported by family and society. Women, on the other hand, are continuously repressed and accused. In the Latin American society, for instance, such a discrepancy is often expressed in the following argument: men are suspected of homosexuality unless they are heterosexually very active, while women, if they were to behave in a similar manner, would be suspected of prostitution. This is why, generally, women feel more responsible, more guilty and dependent than men do, and as a consequence more inclined to suffer from depression. But this is only an apparent condition because if we compare the psychosexual development of both boys and girls, we see that there exists a discrepancy between what we might observe on the surface, and what might exist internally.

Boys generally break the gravitational force exercised by their mothers by identifying with their fathers, who allow and ease the process, helping boys to slowly take their place as males, and from there, to consider the mother as someone very desirable but also forbidden.[1] This condition, however, becomes uncomfortable and dif-

---

[1] Erection difficulties in men are often associated with an early history of seductive or exhibitionistic behavior from the mothers towards their sons, often disguised behind the rationalization

ficult, forcing boys to give it up in adolescence when they search for females outside the family circle in order to avoid being a rival of their fathers, as well as to elude feeling guilty about their incestuous desires. It is, in other words, what Sigmund Freud described as the male Oedipus Complex. But boys usually receive unconditional love from their mothers, because in the process of identification with their fathers, as I just said, they also find a rival. This condition is very different with the female counterpart. Girls receive unconditional love from their mothers, but when they turn towards their fathers, they do not find a rival, but a "seducer" (in the good sense of the word), at least under normal circumstances. In summary, from these observations, we might conclude that boys "get one" and girls "get two." This condition has a determining influence on the character structure of both males and females, in the sense that, deep inside, girls are stronger than boys, and this is why, in general, women can tolerate loneliness better than men. At the same time, the tendency of mothers to identify with their daughters eases the possibility of establishing symbiotic ties with them, a condition that usually translates later on into a greater tendency towards emotional over-reaction and dependency among women, in contrast, with a greater emotional control and better objectivity among men.

During prehistoric ages, the androgenic hormonal forces of males foisted over the estrogenic weakness of females, while at the same time men contemplated—without understanding—the astonishing wonders of maternity, the capacity of women to produce life "all by

---

that this sort of demeanor represents a kind of "openness," or a "natural" way of life.

themselves." The envy, induced by the fact that women were the only ones chosen by the gods to create life (together with the power effected by imprinting), determined men's need to subjugate women. They achieved this not only by the use of their physical strength, but also by the practice of magic, fabricating religions based on masculine supremacy as well as sinful and demonic besmirching of women. This is the origin of the *"Delinquent Eve"* who had no other choice but to support male's ascendancy because at that time muscle power was imperative for survival. "Delinquent Eve," in other words, exalted macho performance in her sons, who then grew and completed the circle by exercising absolute domination over other women, women who used the power of imprinting by means of embellishing themselves and nothing else, never to use any intellectual accomplishment. Women depended so much on the conservation of their body and physical attraction that there was little left for any other talent. In the year 1315, for instance, Clemence of Hungary betrothed herself to Louis X, King of France with great satisfaction, because at the age of twenty-four, she was already considered an old maid.

*Macho men* beget macho men as well as "Delinquent Eves," but feel terrified of the competition and threat exerted by other macho men, and out of phallic rivalry and castration fear, they invented war, using any excuse in order to justify it. At the end of the last century and the beginning of the present one, psychoanalysis helped women to become more aware of their masochistic traits, of their guilt over the power of imprinting, and the fear of their own sexuality. But women have not searched for the answer in themselves; instead they attempted to imitate men, giving place to the appearance of the "Confused Eve," who then generates more aggressive women and more passive men, or in other words, they are responsible for the advent of the *"bisexual generation."* Not long ago, the old time feminist but now masculinist, poet Robert Bly, in a written dialogue with his colleague Keith Thompson, said that he understood the problem with men today, as the existence of a new generation of "soft males," because as he stated, the message proclaimed by feminist women back in the sixties was that these new and strong females only wanted soft males as companions (1982, p. 30). The "solution" to this problem, according to Bly and followers, is to squeeze the "wild man" out of "soft men" during crowded all-male weekend marathons, whose main teaching revolves around imitating all sorts of animals believed to be the expression of a good macho breed, such as wolf or ram. Obviously, "masculinists" searching for their lost male identity by imitating animals is even worse that "feminists" searching for their female identity by imitating men. The problem, I think, is something often seen in this kind of "all to easy," skin deep psychology that pretends to find answers by imitation only, leaving out a serious search of unconscious conflicts and motivations.

The "bisexual generation" will conceivably be more peaceful than the previous "macho generation," avoiding massive confrontations as seen during the last two World Wars, although peace might bring Malthusian predictions about hunger and poverty into the open.[2] Perhaps at this

[2]Thomas Robert Malthus, a British economist, at the end of the eighteenth century shook all the cultivated world of his time when he established that while the population growth followed a

very moment we are witnessing the commencement of a more peaceful generation, with Communism, the Berlin Wall, and the whole USSR's power breaking down, or the changes between a more aggressive Bush and a more congenial Clinton.

Today homosexuality appears to be increasing, either by the increment of more "soft males" (children of "Confused Eves"), because of a greater social acceptance, or both. The rise of homosexuality is not so much an ethical, legal, or moral conflict, or a problem of "homophobia." The real controversy, I think, stems from the fact that a greater acceptance and legalization of homosexuality will threaten the true essence of very important institutions, such as the family, and in years to come even the whole human species. Human beings are the most fragile creatures among all others in the animal kingdom. We require the certainty of a definite equilibrium, the existence of both parents, of a consistent environment that will provide a "holding" environment during infancy's tender years. There is also a great level of suffering among all homosexuals, for the simple reason that every position human beings develop that defies the natural flow of biology will require a significant amount of energy and will demand a great quota of sacrifice in order to sustain that position. Every homosexual rejects his or her own sexuality and usually hopes for the opposite one, and this confusion is always a source of deep suffering, discontent, and low self-steem.

I think, however, that if the partner of the "Delinquent

---

geometrical progression, food grew arithmetically, which in summary signified that if things were to continue in that direction, people might end in cannibalism.

Eve" was the "macho man," and the "bisexual" the companion of the "Confused Eve," the man of the future, engendered by the "Vindicated Eve," will be a more rational kind of person, more apt to share than to impose his androgenic power, and who obviously will be guided by the weight of logic. Couple[3] interaction will be more complementary than competitive, since masculinity will not be considered the opposite of femininity but its complement, its counterpart. Both partners, just by being different, will share and add to the wealth and fascination of their companionship.

---

[3]During the last ten years, Latin Americans are using more often the word *pareja* to designate "a couple," a word that also signifies "equal" or "even."

# 17   VINDICATED EVE

In my vision of the emerging Age of Aquarius, women will
unfold our deepest spiritual potential and create egalitarian
systems of political, economic and social well being for all
citizens of the world.

—Char McKee

The central hypothesis introduced in this essay establishes
that the social profile of humankind depends largely on the
continuous transformation of woman's psychology because she constitutes the beginning of life, the determining
factor that decides, with her imprint and influence, the
outcome of both men and women. Like a never ending
spiral, women will also be affected by science, by new
advances and inventions, as has happened in the past with
the feeding bottle, for instance, or with new forms of
contraceptives, which have been largely responsible for
the increment in their freedom during the present century.

Future discoveries will continue to influence women's psycho-social structure, changing other variables, biological as well as psychological, like menstruation and even maternity, as I stated in previous chapters.

Contraceptives are not a new aspiration of women; they have been in their minds since ancient times. The Egyptians, as well as the Greeks and the Romans, recommended several methods—some absurd and magical, others with a true sense of logic. The most common one was the coitus interruptus, also known as "onanism" because according to the Bible, Onan son of Judah, was ordered by God to procreate with his sister-in-law, but he disobeyed by throwing the "seed" on the floor (Gen. 38:9). In the year 1822, Francis Place, a tailor from London, either entirely overwhelmed by the fifteen children born to his wife, or perhaps tired of sewing so many clothes, or both, got inspired by Malthus' previous predictions about future food shortages and created the order of the "Neo-Malthusian," made up of people who, like Francis, eulogized the need for birth control in order to avoid oncoming famine. But the court magistrates and well-to-do ladies of that time, prompted by forces of Victorian puritanism, accused his and all his friends' ideas of being nothing but pure pornography and finally put all of them behind bars.

Among the first contraceptives to be accepted by the church were the rhythm method and the condom. The latter was believed to be invented by an army Colonel of that name[1]—who never dreamt of his name changing into a "bad" word—on the direct order of King Charles II of

---

[1]Many historians believe the story of a Colonel Condom to be completely uncertain.

England, and living under the shibboleth of "God will never damn a man for allowing himself a little pleasure," wanted some kind of contraception in order to avoid further births of his illegitimate children who were becoming an expensive burden on the kingdom's economy. The first condoms, made of lamb's tripes, were so uncomfortable that people preferred coitus interruptus, until vulcanization was invented in 1839 by Charles Goodyear. But it wasn't until one hundred years later, with the invention of latex, that the condom acquired the consistency as we know it at the present time. Of all the great variety of contraceptives, however, it is the "pill," in all its forms and types, that has contributed the most to women's greater freedom, just as the feeding bottle did by bringing men's help into the picture.

The woman of the future, whom I have named "Vindicated Eve," will have to overcome a multitude of trials in the centuries to come, a very important one being the power of imprinting, which induces such an enormous amount of guilt and creates at the same time a dissociated sexuality, making it difficult for women to become total possessors of their own bodies. Such guilt is absolutely responsible for their almost essential sense of masochism. Once these feelings are conquered, women will abandon the need to imitate men, as we can see now in the "Confused Eve," and will search for their true identity within their own resources, inside the innermost core of their powerful sense of womanhood, what researchers in the field of femininity, such as Merlin Stone, have referred to as the *universal feminine principle.* In general, I say, there are at least two fields whose progress will definitely help women to evolve: one is psychology, the other is electronics. The first will help women to master their own masochism, rescue and be exclusive owners of their bodies, experience the right to their natural power of imprinting, and taste the prerogative of free thinking without the trepidation of sexualized thoughts, which might induce attacks of *epistomophobia*, and so on. The second, electronics, will help women to overcome their estrogenic fragility and allow them to take time off from household chores by producing machines driven by artificial intelligence not requiring any physical strength, which will take over tedious everyday household exigencies.

But the power of imprinting also implies a latent danger of great dimensions, because if such a force is not transcended with time, it might become a real threat. It would give place to a dominion of external and temporary values only, of physical appearance, of just plain body over intellectual achievement, with terrible consequences. I will refer to this predicament in the next chapter.

# 18   BEYOND THE IMPRINTING

> For spirits when they please can either sex assume, or both;
> so soft and uncompounded is their essence.
>
> —John Milton

In the years to come, most of the advance of humanity will hinge on the progress of four different domains: first, *communication and transportation* (electronics); second, *biology and medicine*; third, *social entropy*; and finally, *women*. Of all of these areas, entropy requires some explanation. The concept originated in caloric physics as the Third Law of Thermodynamics, but was also imported to the realm of biology and sociology in order to explain the successive degradation of matter, of energy, as well as societies and cultures, existing or that have existed in the universe, to an ultimate state of uniformity and homogeneity. Recently, we have witnessed the fall of the Berlin

Wall that stood for more than forty-five years. Everyone believed it would be eternal like the Great Wall of China, but the "work" needed by communists to maintain such a division was so strenuous that it could no longer be sustained—like an old refrigerator worn down by its continuous palpitating, facing the incessant beating of entropy, it finally collapsed. This is similar to many Third World country dictators, such as Castro and Saddam Hussein who, like the Berlin Wall, threaten perpetuity. In the immediate future, we will see that the social organization of former communist countries, such as Russia and its allies, will resemble the social structure of socialist Canada or Sweden, among many others, because neither bamboo, nor iron, nor steel curtain, could ever withstand the power of entropy's fatalism: the whole world slowly moves toward uniformity, even in different matters such as nationality, skin color, money, and so forth.

About women: I have already discussed many areas where I think femininity will unfold in the future. The power of imprinting, for instance, carries the risk that the mind may abide by values that are only skin deep, or by the sole weight of youth and external beauty, even more since human beings must face the fatalism of time, aging, and continuous dilapidation of their physical appearance. Although imprinting is implicit and indissoluble in women, forever engraved in the depth of their minds, their bodies age, deteriorate, and progressively lose the attraction and glamour of previous years, from the time of conception and maternity.

The strength that human beings, women in particular, need in order to face the pain induced by such a loss, such a biological and predetermined metamorphosis, depends primarily on the initial infantile sources of love and understanding that the family provided. Many are capable of neutralizing the loss of their youth and reaching an honorable, even intellectually productive old age, while others less fortunate succumb to the uproar of their loss and waste even life itself. The memory is still fresh of the fates of Marilyn Monroe and Elvis Presley, two examples among thousands; at the same time, millions of dollars are being invested in cosmetic industries, plastic surgery, and in the creation of a magic balm that would finally eliminate the traces of the passing years. But in the end only the ingredients of inner wealth, self-esteem, and the capacity to love, particularly in women, will be the constituents that will mitigate and help to overcome the imprinting's absolute and dominant attraction. This transcendence will signify for women an exchange between the force of imprinting they exercised during their youth, and a future project that will provide a real sense of purpose to their life: to generate new life or to achieve the force of intellectual and artistic creativity.

Imprinting is heralded to woman through the eyes of men, where she mirrors herself in men's longing, through the initial image of the younger mother that remains trapped in the unconscious memory of the son. This initial image slowly contrasts with the transformation induced by time and aging, a contrast that recalls, by association, Oscar Wilde's well-known creation *The Picture of Dorian Gray*.[1]

---

[1] It is particularly significant that this issue about the fear of aging and losing the merit of youth was narrated by a male homosexual writer. It is obvious that men also respond to the

Because men blindly obey the power of imprinting, a great importance has been given to physical attraction, anonymously searched for in any woman's body. This induces the risk of using women just as simple objects, instead of the intricate human beings that they are, who palpitate extreme complexity within themselves. For the male, imprinting has no name and he experiences it automatically and indiscriminately with any female. Women, on the other hand, experience men's incapacity to discriminate or to personalize as a particular threat to their relationship and commitment and usually demand the need to be UNIQUE. In other words, the fidelity a woman often requires from her male companion is consequential of the fear she experiences over the fact that he always responds to the imprecise and anonymous demand of imprinting in the body of *any woman: just any "chick."*

In conclusion, a woman will demand to be the only

---

need to beautify their bodies, most of all homosexuals and those of a narcissistic nature. We know, since Freud's time, that the human soul in general is bisexual and that only the predominance of one gender over the other will at the end guarantee any specific identity. When I say that men also like to embellish themselves, I think that what they try to adorn is the feminine part within themselves, which represents some of the women's power of imprinting that might have been subtracted and incorporated by men during childhood. Men try to embellish whatever they might feel as feminine in themselves. Men's envy over women's power of imprinting can be observed in the different fashion styles they have used throughout history, such as in the French court during the seventeen and eighteen hundreds, or as seen today in many male youth's modern fashions: long hair, earrings, clothing, and so on.

and specific object of her companion's desire as a compensation for two threats: *In the first place, the force of imprinting slipping away due to aging, and secondly, the fear of knowing themselves, not as unique, but as an indefinite and imprecise object within the core of men's desire.* Women will always allude to a man as a person, by his name, but men often refer to a woman as an object, usually a part of her anatomy: "a piece of tail," a "chick," and in Spanish, "an ass."

Faithfulness usually represents a demand that appears within the heart of a couple, as a need to preserve its continuity. Faithfulness, in general, is easier for women because their desire towards men is not so much based on imprinting, that is, on the attractiveness of their bodies. For the same reason, women are more ready to accept the aging of their male companions, while men, responding to the call of imprinting, always have a preference for a younger body. Often couples break up at the level of their middle age, when the woman's physique has already languished and no longer discloses or resembles, in man's eyes, the image of his younger mother. A mature woman's search for a young man usually portrays a compensation for the painful feeling of having lost the force of imprinting, because she wishes to revive the freshness of previous times mirrored in the young man's longing. Usually a woman prefers the company of a man older than herself, perhaps unconsciously wishing for the presence of a protective father image—different from the male, who often favors just the splendor of physical beauty. Women, on the other hand, are generally very preoccupied with what other women are wearing, carefully inspecting them while at the same time, either with envy or contempt, comparing make-up, anatomy, or attire, matching imprinting with obvious competition. In social gatherings, for instance, men usually share the same type of clothing, as if they welcome sameness; but women, on the other hand, might go into a complete fit if, by any stroke of bad luck, they were to meet someone dressed in exactly the same kind of outfit. Women cannot overcome the threat of anonymity that imprinting power has equally provided them, looking very much alike in the eyes of all men, who only discriminate between younger and older bodies. This is why every woman in the entire world is caught in what I have named the *"imprinting trap,"* meaning the need to exalt and sustain the power of imprinting by beautifying themselves, while having to avoid at any cost the terror of anonymity. This is why all women, regardless of their age, social status, culture, color, size, or language, have this tremendous need to buy clothing and spend hour after hour endlessly searching in stores, while most men would be bored to death—unless they have some feminine identification—under the same circumstances.

The *"imprinting trap"* also implies a complicated chain of associated events: in the first place, women's bodies are, because of imprinting, particularly sexualized, encumbering women with the burden, already present in Genesis, that they are absolutely responsible for any seduction.[2] In the second place, such sexualization makes women's freedom suspicious of being libertine, inducing, as a compensation, dependency, guilt, and masochism. In

---

[2]This is why it is so difficult for women in general to prove themselves innocent during legal prosecution about rape or any other kind of male sexual harassment.

the third place, and very importantly, total sexualization of all of their actions induces a fear of thinking, or "epistemo-phobia," that prevents women from reasoning or using their intellectual endowment in order to free themselves from such fatalism. Future women must overcome this dilemma in order to avoid, in Susan Faludi's words, "back-lashes" and be able to reach their full potentiality and to finally achieve the determining social role they will defi-nitely play someday in future history. Hopefully men will encourage them, because without their participation these changes might be very difficult.

As new psychoanalytical discoveries evolve and shed new light on the internal development of women, a sort of geometrical, or hopefully spiral progression, will work its way to generate better mothers who will then produce better children, and who will eventually become better parents. Future transformation of mankind is both cause and consequence of women's psychic transfiguration. Mothers will be more accepting and understanding of their daughters early sexuality, their right to their own bodies, to play, discover, and achieve orgasm through masturba-tion.

What Wilfred Bion has referred to as the "continent mother," as well as Donald Winnicott when he spoke of the "good enough mother," was the mother's capacity to provide a "metabolizing" and understanding kind of love to her children: a mother capable of helping them to incorporate inside of them a healthy world filled with comprehension, trust, self-confidence, love, understanding of themselves and of others, and as a consequence, have the capacity to forgive and have compassion. I think it is very important at this moment to distinguish between several basic human feelings, such as sexuality, passion, need, love and trust, because *sex is instinct, passion is immediate and intense, need is selfish, love means history and freedom, while trust is the capacity for renunciation.*

*Love* must be differentiated from need because both may appear similar in their form of expression, but are completely the opposite in their final purpose. Love means to be aware of the other, as someone different from oneself, as a complete human being who cannot be possessed and by whom we cannot be possessed either. It means to help and encourage the other to reach his or her potentiality, to unconditionally provide the other with what they want. Love always elapses within the boundary of absolute freedom and is always a voluntary decision that arouses unrestrained without any other alternative. Love is particular, personal, private, and never anonymous. *Need*, on the other hand, determines the action between parent and child, between master and slave; it imprisons and suffocates the person, and is always the expression of a deep feeling of fear, dependency, insecurity, and spiritual disadvantage. Love allows us to share, without losing our autonomy or identity, in complete freedom of expression and in full power of our actions, while need shatters the boundaries between oneself and the other, inducing symbiosis and maintaining the primitive infantile relationship between the mother and her child. *Love liberates but need oppresses.*

Several circumstances inhibit the spontaneous flow of love—the capacity to love freely without restrictions—and these are usually the same reasons for which we cannot love ourselves either. This condition is due to the inner presence of an extremely demanding unconscious attitude that often reaches the level of a primitive inner sado-masochism, of man against himself, which depends, of course, on the manner in which we were raised. Freud referred to this moralistic, internal attitude, or mental "agency" (to use psychoanalytical terminology), at the beginning of his discoveries as a "moral consciousness" and later as the well-known "super-ego." This conscious-ness forces us, without realizing, to split the world into black and white, good and bad, perfect and imperfect. We are then led to reject our imperfections and project them onto others, in the form of continuous criticism; in other words, any little fault becomes a disaster. Such a need for perfection, of course, is completely irrational, representing among many other things, a confusion between the parts and the whole; it is something like getting rid of your car when it has a flat tire because it is no longer perfect. The same stance is held in relation to people, since we are inclined to reject them once we have found their "normal" imperfections. This gives rise to the well-known dilemma of rejecting those who want us and wanting those who reject us.

Love is capable of growing only where there is imper-fection, and will always be contaminated because it em-braces the totality of the persons involved, with their good and with their bad. It cannot blossom unless it comprises in its essence the spirit of forgiveness and compassion. Love also requires history, is built step-by-step in time, and grows imperceptibly like grass. It is constructed with details, with the same material that dreams and memories are made of, and hurts with the same moderation and the same hope because as always, those who love know that they are loved too.

*Passion,* on the other hand, has no history; it is immediate, explosive, intense. Everything is perfect and marvelous because there is no room for defects; if any fault were to appear, passion immediately fades away. Imperfection is the executioner of passion.

*Sex* is pure instinct, plain animality. It is almost foreign to us, like a drug where only pleasure in the form of orgasm is important. Without any conscious election, it is determined by the forces of nature previously organized with that sole purpose. Just like life and death about which nobody ever consulted us, it is there and forces us, regardless, to its final satisfaction. This is even more so in the case of sexual deviations or perversions, where sex becomes the main intention, the only purpose, like a genetic parasite that imprisons the mind and body and forces the person to repeat the act compulsively. The great complication of sexual perversion is not so much the act in itself, which might involve different forms of making love outside conventional ones; on the contrary, sex has implicit in it such a tendency to monotony that any creativity is always welcome. The problem with perversions is exactly the opposite, the need to repeat exactly the same thing, over and over, without any creativity or ever being satisfied, making it extremely boring for someone who does not participate in the same kind of perversion.[3] Nobody is completely free from the determining factors already es-

---

[3]This particular situation was illustrated some time ago in the well-known movie *9½ Weeks.*

tablished during childhood. We might think that we are choosing our sexual and marital companions according to pure chance, and refuse to accept that most of our behavior has been decided according to scripts recorded in the innermost corner of our unconscious minds.

If the hypothesis introduced in this essay communicates a certain truth and makes some evolutionary or historical sense, we could then imagine that many years will have to elapse for women to feel the right over their imprinting without having to experience any sign of remorse. Having reached this position, they can peacefully start to transcend it, and find their true inner values. How many years must go by if women, just beginning the "Confused Eve" era, have barely begun to question their own masochism?

I predict, with Nostradamus's consent, that some time in the future, women, transformed into the image of "Vindicated Eve," will introduce men and women to earthly Paradise. Paradise is not a myth from the past, nor is it a myth from Genesis: it has never existed but in the fantasy of ancient people who wisely apprehended it inside their own "selfness," within the mysterious spark and abysmal magic of the human "collective unconscious." *Paradise is just a myth; it has never existed, but perhaps it might be a reality in the future.* "Vindicated Eve" might arrive many years from now as a well resolute "Sara",[4] who, as a new Messiah, will rescue men from castration. Maybe then we might understand that *GOD IS A WOMAN.*

---

[4]I believe that the series of new movies based on the "Terminator" have some relation to this kind of fantasy, but with a violent male macho type of orientation, which is not what I have in mind here.

# References

Bly, R., Thompson, K. (May 1982). What Men Really Want: A New Age Interview with Robert Bly. *New Age*, p. 30.

Bowlby, J. (1969). *Attachment and Loss*, Vol. I, p. 223. New York: Basic Books.

Cardinal, M. (1976). *Las Palabras Para Decirlo*, p. 14. Barcelona: Editorial Noguera.

Charen, M. (March 23, 1984). The Feminist Mistake. *National Review*, p. 24.

Douglas, A. (1977). *The Feminization of American Culture*. New York: Avon Books.

Eisler, R. (1989). Reclaiming Our Goddess Heritage: The Feminine Principle in Our Past and Future. In *The Goddess Rewakening*, p. 27. New York: Quest Books.

Faludi, S. (1991). *Backlash*. New York: Doubleday.

Friday, N. (1991). *Women on Top*. New York: Pocket Star Books.

Leonelly, E. (1984). *Mas Allá de los Labios.* Barcelona: Editorial Noguera.

Lyndon, S. (1970). The Politics of Orgasm. In *Sisterhood is Powerful.* New York: Random House.

Morgan, R. (1970). Introduction. In *Sisterhood is Powerful,* p. xvi. New York: Random House.

Ortega y Gasset, J. (1961). El Hombre y la Gente. In *Obras Completas, Vol. 7,* p. 71. Madrid: Revista de Oriente.

Schwartz, K. (1985). *The Male Member.* New York: Martin Press.

Spender, D. (1983). *Feminist Theorists: Three Centuries of Key Women Thinkers.* New York: Pantheon Books.

Stone, M. (1989). Introduction. In *The Goddess Reawakening,* p. 2, ed. S. Nicholson. New York: Quest Books.

Taylor, J. (1991). Don't Blame Me: The New Culture of Victimization. In *Backlash,* p. 28. New York: Doubleday.

Tevlin, J. (Nov.–Dec. 1989). *Of Hawks and Men: A Weekend in the Male Wilderness,* p. 50. Utne Reader.

Unamuno, M. (1912). El Sentimiento Trágico de la Vida. In *Obras Selectas,* p. 333. Madrid: Editorial Plenitud.

# INDEX